CONVENIENTLY
VEGAN

ALSO BY DEBRA WASSERMAN

Simply Vegan
(With Reed Mangels, Ph.D., R.D.)

The Lowfat Jewish Vegetarian Cookbook

Meatless Meals for Working People
(With Charles Stahler)

No Cholesterol Passover Recipes
(With Charles Stahler)

This book is dedicated to the memory of my Uncle Leonard Weintraub. Your positive outlook on life and passion for urban gardening will always be remembered.

CONVENIENTLY VEGAN

Turn Packaged Foods into Delicious Vegetarian Dishes

By Debra Wasserman

The Vegetarian Resource Group
Baltimore, Maryland

A NOTE TO THE READER

The contents of *Conveniently Vegan* are not intended to provide personal medical advice. Medical advice should be obtained from a qualified health professional.

© Copyright 1997, Revised 1999, Debra Wasserman
Published by The Vegetarian Resource Group,
PO Box 1463, Baltimore, Maryland 21203.

Cover artwork and illustrations by John Peters

Library of Congress Cataloging-in-Publication Data
Conveniently Vegan — Turn Packaged Foods into
Delicious Vegetarian Dishes/Debra Wasserman
Library of Congress Catalog Card Number: 97-60064

ISBN 0-931411-18-1

Printed in the United States of America
10 9 8 7 6 5 4 3 2

CONTENTS

FOREWORD

The idea for this book came to me almost five years ago as a result of several encounters I had with shoppers at my local supermarket and natural foods store. It seemed as if every time I went grocery shopping a customer or two would notice me grabbing items such as bulgur, couscous, tofu, bok choy, mangos, or acorn squash. Next, the individual(s) would question me as to how I prepared the item(s). I offered suggestions and soon others became interested in our conversation. I quickly realized consumers now had access to a wide variety of natural foods in almost any store they shopped; however, little if any instruction as to how to cook these products was offered.

Today, many large supermarkets stock even a wider variety of natural foods including vegan hot dogs and burgers, quinoa and basmati rice, organic canned tomato products, numerous types of flour, fresh herbs, exotic fruits and vegetables, plus so much more. However, mainstream supermarkets and even some natural foods stores still fail to teach their shoppers how to use this terrific array of foods.

Conveniently Vegan helps fill this educational gap. I have been vegan for over 18 years and throughout this period I created new recipes and cooked with a tremendous variety of foods. Back when I was a child, supermarkets did not so much as offer whole wheat flour or brown rice. Fortunately, my family belonged to a buying club where a group of families ordered natural foods together and received a discount. Whole grains, legumes, and a wide range of produce have long been staples in my diet.

Beginning cooks and those with years of experience preparing vegetarian meals will find much to learn in this book. Along with useful information there are 150 vegan recipes made from packaged natural foods products containing no animal ingredients. Most of the dishes can be prepared quickly. A nutritional breakdown is offered after each recipe, too.

To do my research I visited supermarkets, natural foods stores, and ethnic and gourmet shops throughout the United States and parts of Canada. I also attended natural products shows in both countries. I carried a list of all the vegan natural foods products I had found and added new items as I located them. While searching for these products, I also created a list of companies manufacturing and/or distributing each item. This list found near the end of *Conveniently Vegan* may be helpful if you are unable to locate a certain product in the store where you regularly shop. Most supermarkets have some type of informational counter where requests are made to stock items. Knowing the name of the manufacturer and city and state where the product is made can help the buyers locate the item(s) you desire. Don't forget to purchase the product(s) once they appear on your store's shelves so that they remain stocked.

Finally, one of my goals in this book is to help the reader enjoy shopping and cooking. Natural foods stores and supermarkets are continuously adding new and exciting products. Now is the perfect time for you and your family and friends to experience some of these new foods.

ACKNOWLEDGMENTS

Writing a book is always a huge undertaking. It is even more so when you are Co-Director of The Vegetarian Resource Group (VRG), a national non-profit educational organization. This book would not exist if it were not for the help and support of numerous people. First, I would like to thank Reed Mangels, Ph.D., R.D., for devoting numerous hours (often very late at night after her two young daughters have gone to bed) in her hectic schedule to provide the nutritional breakdowns found after each recipe in this book. Reed offered valuable suggestions throughout the years I worked on this book. I also greatly appreciate the illustrations and cover art drawn by John Peters. Your talent shines throughout this book.

Secondly, I want to thank Michele Cagan, Eva Mossman, and Israel Mossman for volunteering to edit and proofread the text. The three of you spent a tremendous number of hours on this task and contributed greatly to this final product.

I would also like to thank VRG staff members whose hard work and dedication each day helps enable me to find the time to work on books such as this one. Several of you offered advice while I chugged away on this book and others taste-tested recipes. Thanks to Brad Scott, who lent his computer expertise to make this project happen. Special appreciation goes to Charles Stahler, who put up with me when the pressures of everyday life and completing this book often became overwhelming. Your recommendations and constant support are treasured.

Finally, I would like to thank my parents for encouraging all three of their children to take risks and be creative. Life would never be this fun and exciting if it were not for your upbringing.

INTRODUCTION

The natural foods industry is an important and growing phenomenon in the total food market. For many people, eating natural foods is a new and exciting experience. However, to these same individuals many of the foods are unfamiliar and thus intimidating. This book offers tremendous help to those people as well as experienced natural foods consumers.

MEAT NO LONGER MAKES THE MEAL

Not too long ago, the average shopper felt that a meal must contain some type of meat to make it a real feast. Today, this is no longer true for a large segment of our population. People of all walks of life and from all age groups are making vegetarian products a more frequent part of their overall diet. In some cases these individuals are becoming full-fledged vegetarians or vegans.

In 1994, a study commissioned by Land O' Lakes reported that over half of all American households ate two or more meatless dinners each week and 20 percent of U.S. households ate four or more meatless dinners per week. This same report stated that the meat is being replaced by vegetables (60%), pasta (41%), beans (16%), and rice (14%). These staples are often mixed with sauces, dressings, and other toppings to make exquisite meals.

SUPERMARKETS AND OTHER STORES RESPOND TO NEW DIETARY TRENDS

Today's cooks searching for vegetarian foods are more likely than ever to be doing their food shopping at their local supermarket or, in some instances, a natural foods supermarket. According to a report titled "Natural Products Industry Snapshot" (released by Boulder, Colorado based New Hope Communications in March 1996), a 22.6% sales increase in 1995 pushed overall sales of natural and organic products to $9.17 billion. Organic sales alone reached $2.8 billion, an increase of 21.7%. Since 1991, the natural products industry has seen double-digit growth.

This same report indicated that there are approximately 136,000 mainstream stores across the United States and estimates are that up to 80% of these stores carry some natural products. The survey also states that there are approximately 6,600 natural/health food stores in this country. This figure includes the natural foods supermarket chains such as Whole Foods and Wild Oats.

A recent survey conducted by RLB Food Distributors located in West Caldwell, New Jersey, polled 150 supermarket executives. The report revealed that an overwhelming 91% of those supermarkets polled indicated that their stores will sell more organic products in the future. Respondents also were asked to predict the three most important ways in which supermarkets will be different in five years. The most common responses included better customer service, more prepared meals, more organic and natural foods, higher quality and service, in-house restaurants, and child-care areas.

Another poll conducted in 1995 by the Food Marketing Institute (FMI), a Washington-based trade association for grocery and supermarket retailers, indicated that nearly 51% of the senior management at mainstream supermarkets believed that natural foods would become very important to their company by 1996. Indeed, most shoppers have witnessed these changes and are certain to continue to see more products added.

Mainstream retailers are still unsure of where to place these natural foods products inside their stores. About 60% integrate natural products with traditional items, while about 40% have separate natural products sections. As a result, shoppers are often unaware of the availability of natural foods products in mainstream supermarkets simply because they cannot locate them.

MANUFACTURERS PRODUCE MORE CONVENIENCE FOODS

So often I have heard people say that they would love to become vegetarian but it's too difficult. Fortunately, this perception is rapidly being torn apart. Natural foods manufacturers have responded to demand by offering a wide variety of convenience foods. Many of these foods are vegan (they contain no animal products including meat, poultry, fish, dairy products, eggs, or honey). Today, natural foods stores and many supermarkets offer a wide selection of quick and easy natural foods products that you can turn into a delicious meal.

For example, in the produce section of any supermarket you will no longer find only one variety of mushroom. Instead, you may see portabello and/or shiitake mushrooms. If you are lucky, you will also find organic produce and an excellent selection of fresh herbs. In the refrigerator cases you might find tofu, whole wheat tortillas without animal fat, and occasionally vegan cheese and soy yogurt. Move to the meat section next, and you may be surprised to find fat-free vegan hot dogs situated between all the meat hot dogs. On other shelves you will see grains such as barley, couscous, quinoa, bulgur, brown rice, and basmati rice. Some supermarkets now stock organic canned tomato products and beans including chickpeas, black beans, kidney beans, pinto beans, and others. You will also find dried legumes including lentils and yellow split peas. The availability of natural foods products is endless. *Conveniently Vegan* will demonstrate how easy it is to prepare dishes with these products.

WHAT YOU WILL FIND IN CONVENIENTLY VEGAN

In *Conveniently Vegan* I offer definitions of many of the natural foods products and new produce items found in grocery stores today. This section tells you what the items are, how they look and are packaged, and ways in which they can be prepared. Therefore, the next time you see acorn or butternut squash, barley, couscous, bulgur, veggie hot dogs, tofu, seitan (wheat gluten), and soy milk, or canned organic beans and tomato products, you will feel comfortable purchasing and preparing meals with these foods.

Secondly, menu suggestions are given for breakfast, lunch, and dinner. These ideas certainly make meal planning a lot easier. The menus are followed by information on how you can determine the amount of fat you are consuming each day, as well as a list of recipes in this book containing large amounts of calcium and/or iron.

Next, you will find 150 vegan recipes using packaged natural foods along with fresh fruit, vegetables, and herbs. Each recipe centers around at least one packaged natural foods item. These products can be purchased in boxes, cans, jars, or bags and may be fresh, frozen, canned, or dried. Some stores offer some of these foods in bins which minimizes excess packaging. You should also purchase organic products when available and, of course, recycle. Organic canned items are often lower in sodium than other brands. Many of us desire convenience foods today, but if you have the time, beans can be cooked from scratch in large amounts, then frozen in small batches for future use.

Many of the recipes in this book are quick and easy to prepare and are perfect if you have a hectic lifestyle. Some necessitate a longer cooking or baking time. Most of the recipes are made with one or two pots or pans, making cleaning up a simple task. If you live alone, in most cases you can quickly divide the recipes in half or in fourths to meet your needs. In some cases, leftovers can be brought to work or school the next day for a delicious meal. Finally, throughout the book I have made a point to indicate which recipes children will enjoy.

CONVENIENTLY VEGAN MAKES IT EASY TO MEET THE U.S. DIETARY GUIDELINES

In 1995, the United States issued new dietary guidelines. These guidelines provide advice for healthy Americans, two years and older, about food choices that promote health and prevent disease. Individuals are encouraged to choose a wide variety of foods from the base of the U.S. Department of Agriculture's Food Guide Pyramid. The pyramid shows that foods from the grain group, along with vegetables and fruits, are the basis of healthful diets. These are the very foods that form the foundation of a healthy vegan diet. Each day you should choose most of your calories from foods in the grain group (6-11 servings), the vegetable group (3-5 servings), and the fruit group (2-4 servings).

What is considered a serving? In the grain group, 1 slice of bread, 1 ounce of ready-to-eat cereal, and 1/2 cup of cooked cereal, rice, and pasta is equivalent to one serving. In the vegetable group, 1 cup of raw leafy vegetables, 1/2 cup of other vegetables (cooked or chopped raw), and 3/4 cup of vegetable juice is considered a serving. In the fruit group, 1 medium apple, banana, or orange, 1/2 cup of chopped, cooked, or canned fruit, and 3/4 cup of fruit juice is equal to a serving. Recipes in *Conveniently Vegan* are divided into categories to make it easy for the reader to consume foods in all food groups. You will find grain, bean, pasta, vegetable, and meat alternative sections containing both main dishes and side dishes.

According to this report, "Vegetarian diets are consistent with the Dietary Guidelines and can meet Recommended Dietary Allowances (RDA) for nutrients." Vegans must supplement their diets with a source of vitamin B12. This daily requirement can be met by consuming fortified breakfast cereals such as Grape-Nuts cereal (1/2 cup supplies the adult RDA), Red Star T-6635+ nutritional yeast (1-2 teaspoons supplies the adult RDA), or other fortified vegan foods such as some brands of veggie burgers.

One last point — try to find time for exercise and relaxation. This is as important as a healthy diet.

Some of the following vegan foods may be new to you
or your family, while others you may use already.

FRUITS AND VEGETABLES

Produce sections of grocery stores today are overflowing with new and exciting items. Be sure to try many of these delicious fruits and vegetables.

Acorn Squash (Table Queen) is an oval shaped winter squash usually 4 to 7 inches long and weighing 1 to 2 pounds. It has a dark green ribbed skin that often is streaked with yellow or orange. Its flesh is yellow/ orange. Acorn squash can be baked, cooked or steamed, and mashed. Stuffed acorn squash is decorative on any table.

Avocados (Alligator Pears) have been popular in Central and South America since the third century B.C.E. In the 1800s, the Spaniards brought them to the United States. Today avocados are grown in several different varieties in California, Florida, Africa, and the Mediterranean region. Avocados have a light-green flesh with a large seed and dark green, rough, leathery skin. To ripen avocados, simply place them in a paper bag and store them at room temperature until soft. Avocado is most commonly used to prepare guacamole and salad dressings, but can also be used to prepare sandwiches and salads.

Bok Choy (Chinese White Cabbage) is an Oriental vegetable that is similar to, but milder in taste than, cabbage. It has snow-white stalks, a slightly bulbous base, and dark green leaves. Some say it resembles Swiss chard. Hong Kong farmers grow over twenty different varieties. In the United States about five different kinds of bok choy are available. You can used bok choy in place of cabbage in many dishes or even to replace celery in some recipes.

Brussels Sprouts are actually wild cabbage having stems covered with heads of miniature cabbages. They originated in Northern Europe. You can cook or steam Brussels Sprouts or stir-fry them.

Butternut Squash looks like a pear-shaped bottle with a long neck. It is a winter squash and is yellow to buff. The flesh is orange and very sweet. Butternut squash can be steamed and mashed or baked. When cooked you can eat its rind, too. Add butternut squash to soup, chili, stews, and casseroles.

Capers are small and round in shape. They are dark green and usually sold pickled in jars. Capers are actually flower buds of the caper bush found in the Mediterranean and parts of Asia. Use capers in sauces and dressings, and on pizza, salads, etc.

Chinese Cabbage (Napa Cabbage, Pe-tsai) is a large lettuce-like vegetable native to China but grown also in the United States and elsewhere. Its outer leaves are long and green. Chinese cabbage can be served raw in salads or pickled. You can also stuff the leaves or sauté the cabbage.

Collard Greens (Collards) are large, dark green, smooth leaves. They are a variety of cabbage that doesn't form a head. They are native to eastern Mediterranean countries and grow mostly in the southern section of the United States. They are high in calcium. Use collard greens in soups and stir-fry dishes.

Dates are sweet, oblong fruits of the date palm. They contain a narrow hard seed. Dates grew in the Holy Land over 8,000 years ago. Egypt is the biggest producer of dates. They grow in clusters of up to 200 dates weighing up to 25 pounds. Use fresh or dried dates in desserts, salads, and in grain-based dishes.

Jalapeño Peppers are deep green and about 2 inches long. These peppers originated in Mexico and many are grown in Texas. Jalapleño peppers are hot and commonly used to prepare Mexican dishes.

Kale is the ruffled or crinkled leaf of a variety of cabbage whose leaves are green, reddish, or purple. Unlike cabbage, the leaves do not form a tight head. Kale is native to eastern Mediterranean countries and is grown in parts of the United States. It is high in calcium and can be steamed and added to soups, stir-fries, soups, and sauces.

Kiwi (Chinese Gooseberry) was called young tao and highly prized by the court of the great Khans in southern China. By the 19th century, the English cultivated kiwi under the name Chinese gooseberry. Once cultivated in New Zealand, they were called kiwi after the native birds there. Kiwi are now grown in California. They are oval in shape with fuzzy brown skin. The fruit is light green and sweet containing tiny edible black seeds. Use kiwi to prepare shakes, desserts, and fruit salads.

Mandarin Oranges when canned are satsuma oranges. These miniature oranges are from China. Look for varieties packed in their own juice. Use mandarin oranges in fruit shakes and salads.

Mangos grow on tropical or sub-tropical trees and have been enjoyed in India for over 4,000 years. Unripe mango flesh is green and used in chutneys and preserves. Ripe mangoes are red and soft with an orange-yellow flesh. They are very sweet. Mangoes can be used to prepare fruit shakes, salads, salsas, salad dressings, and desserts.

Okra is a green pod that grows on tall tropical and semi-tropical plants. Okra is native to Africa and is sometimes referred to as gumbo in the United States. It becomes sticky when cooked and gives thickness to dishes, in addition to flavor. Okra is delicious served alone or in soups, stews, Cajun dishes, and stir-fry dishes.

Pimentos are the ripe red fruit of a mild, sweet pepper plant. Pimentos are used in relishes and sauces and are often stuffed in olives. Use pimentos in dips and spreads, salads, and pasta dishes.

Portabello Mushrooms (Roma Mushrooms) are from Italy. Their large caps resemble the shape and size of a small pancake. Their stems are long and thick. You can make delicious grilled Portabello mushroom sandwiches, stuff them, or use these mushrooms in any dish calling for mushrooms.

Prunes are dried sweet plums. They look like large raisins and are an excellent source of iron and fiber. Prunes can be eaten as is or stewed. Use prunes to prepare stuffing, compotes, and desserts.

Savoy Cabbage has a large, compact head and curly, crinkled green leaves. Its name comes from the Savoy region of France. Use Savoy cabbage for stuffed cabbage and to prepare cole slaw, salads, etc.

Scallions (Spring Onions) are young tender onions which are harvested before their bulbs enlarge. They are green in color with tiny white bulbs. Scallions are generally mild and both the white stem and green tops are eaten raw or cooked. They are terrific in salads, soups, and stir-fry dishes.

Shiitake Mushrooms (Forest, Black Forest, Golden Oak, Oriental Black, or Chinese Black Mushrooms) are fleshy, gold to brown in color, parasol-like in shape, and should be firm, dry, and meaty in texture. Shiitake mushrooms can be grilled, broiled, or stir-fried. Use these mushrooms to prepare soups, sandwiches, and casseroles.

Snow Peas are tiny green peas in flat thin pods. They are so tender that the pod is eaten together with the peas. Snow peas are popular in Chinese cookery and can be purchased fresh and frozen. Add snow peas to soups and stir-fries.

Water Chestnuts are corms, underwater stem tips, from which a kind of water grass sprouts. Water chestnuts have a sweet crispness like coconut and are an off-white color. They are popular in Asian cuisine and are called ma tai in the Cantonese dialect of Chinese. Use water chestnuts in salads, stir-fries, and stews.

Watercress is a creeping perennial herb of the mustard family. It grows in springs or in clear, cool streams. Watercress can be tossed into salads, stir-fried with garlic, steamed, or added to soups.

Yams are infrequently found in American markets since they are native to Asia and West Africa. However, a variety of the sweet potato with a deep orange color is sold in the United States. It can be boiled, baked, or used in chili, stews, and casseroles.

Yellow Squash is a summer squash that has a yellow rind and white flesh. Its shape resembles zucchini, but it has a milder flavor. Use yellow squash in soups, stews, casseroles, and stir-fries.

Zucchini (Courgette, Marrow) is a very dark green summer squash having a long, slightly curved cylindrical shape. It is of Italian origin. You can simply steam or stir-fry zucchini or use it raw in salads. You can also use zucchini in soups or stuff and bake them.

GRAINS

Grains can be purchased in bulk food bins at many natural food stores as well as at many large supermarkets. A variety of packaged grains can also be found in grocery stores, especially in those with an ethnic food or natural food section. Gourmet and ethnic shops also commonly offer a variety of grains. In general, whole grains will have more fiber than those that are more refined.

Amaranth is a tiny, yellow-brown grain that dates back over 6,000 years ago and is tied closely to the Aztec Indians of Mexico. Traditionally, the seeds have been popped, milled, and used to make flatbread, prepared as cereal, or mixed with a sweetener to make a dessert. To yield about 2-1/4 cups of amaranth, cook 1 cup of raw amaranth in 3 cups of liquid for about 20 minutes. Amaranth can be used as a cooked cereal for breakfast or to replace rice in some dishes such as salads, soups, and pilafs.

Barley is a small white grain with a thin brown line running down the center. It originated in North Africa and Asia. Hulled barley is higher in fiber than pearled barley; however, most barley found in American stores is pearled. To yield about 3-1/2 cups of barley, cook 1 cup of raw barley in 3 cups of liquid for about 1 hour. Barley has a mild taste and chewy texture. It can be used in cereals, soups, salads, baked goods, burgers, stews, casseroles, puddings, or as a substitute for rice in recipes.

Basmati Rice (Calmati, Kasmati, Texmati) is a particularly flavorful long-grain rice often used to prepare Indian cuisine. Authentic basmati is imported from India and Pakistan and has a nutty aroma. Domestic versions are now sold and are available as either white or brown basmati. Cooking instructions can be found on the package. Use basmati rice in soups, salads, pilafs, and burgers.

Brown Rice is the whole rice kernel from which only the outer hull has been removed. It is available in short, medium, and long grain varieties. Brown rice takes longer to cook then white rice. To yield about 3 cups of brown rice, cook 1 cup raw brown rice in 2-1/2 cups of liquid for about 50 minutes. Use brown rice in soups, salads, stuffing, burgers, casseroles, and desserts.

Bulgur (Wheat Pilaf) is made from wheat berries that have been pearled, steamed, dried, and then cracked and toasted. It is the bran and germ of wheat grain. Bulgur is a staple in Eastern Europe and the Middle East. To yield about 2-1/2 cups of bulgur, cook 1 cup of raw bulgur in 2-1/2 cups liquid for about 20 minutes. Bulgur can be used to thicken pasta sauces or added to chili recipes. Bulgur also can be used to make loaves, burgers, salads, soups, stuffing, pilafs, stews, casseroles, and puddings.

Cornmeal is coarsely ground corn and is usually either yellow or white. Blue cornmeal is sold in southwestern United States. Use cornmeal in cakes, breads, pancakes, and desserts.

Couscous is made from durum wheat which has been ground, steamed, and dried. It can be purchased in refined and whole grain varieties and is a very popular Middle Eastern, North African, and Mediterranean staple. The couscous available in the United States is usually made from semolina wheat, a type of durum wheat used in pasta. Couscous cooks quickly and can be used to prepare salads, to stuff vegetables, to replace the rice in some recipes, or to make puddings or cakes.

Farfel is a noodle-like mixture of flour and water shaped like small pellets. Look for this product in the Kosher food section of your favorite store. Be sure to purchase eggless farfel and use it to prepare soups, stews, and stuffing.

Matzo Meal is unleavened bread (matzo) that has been finely ground. It is commonly used during the Jewish holiday of Passover. Matzo meal can often replace fine bread crumbs in a recipe and is delicious in stuffing.

Millet is a tiny, round grain which is yellow and popular in Indian, African, and some Asian cooking. A trick to cooking millet is first to toast it until it's lightly brown and emits an aroma. To yield about 3-1/2 cups of millet, cook 1 cup of raw millet in 3 cups of liquid for about 40 minutes. Millet can be used in cereals, soups, stuffing, pilafs, burgers, stews, casseroles, and puddings.

Oats in the form of steel-cut oats are a staple of Scotland, Ireland, and northern England. Rolled oats are oat grains which have been hulled, softened by steam, and then pressed flat. They can be used as a hot cereal and in granola, to thicken soups and stews, as a binder in burgers and loaves, or to prepare baked goods including crusts.

Oriental Cellophane Noodles (Bean Threads) are Chinese in origin and are sold in nest-like swirls. They are made from the starch of the mung bean. Cellophane noodles are clear and vary in thickness, although most are quite thin. Soak these noodles in hot water rather than boiled water to prepare. Use cellophane noodles in soups, casseroles, or stews.

Quinoa (pronounced *keen-wah)* is a small seed. Technically, it is not a cereal grain but a fruit. It has been cultivated by the Incas of South America in the Andes for at least 5,000 years and has a delicious nutty flavor. To yield 3 cups of quinoa, cook 1 cup of raw quinoa in 2 cups of liquid for about 20 minutes. Use quinoa to make a cooked breakfast cereal, to make a salad or stuff vegetables, to prepare vegetable patties or croquettes, or to replace rice in some dishes.

Somen Noodles are white or beige Japanese noodles made of wheat flour and are cut thinner than Udon noodles. As a result they also cook more quickly than Udon noodles. Use somen noodles in soups, stir-fries, or to replace other pasta in dishes.

Udon Noodles are beige or cream-colored Japanese noodles that are thicker than Somen noodles, flat, and made from wheat or brown rice flour. Use Udon noodles in salads or in place of linguine in dishes.

Wild Rice is actually the seed of an aquatic grass and is native to the Great Lakes region of the United States. It is quite expensive and therefore it is often sold mixed with another grain. To yield 3-1/2 cups of wild rice, cook 1 cup raw wild rice in 3-1/2 cups liquid for at least 1 hour. Wild rice grains are larger than rice and can be used alone or with other grains in pilafs, salads, and soups, or to stuff vegetables.

LEGUMES

Beans can be purchased precooked in cans from natural food stores as well as supermarkets, gourmet shops, and ethnic food stores. Rinsing canned beans prior to using them can reduce their sodium content by 40-50%. Several organic varieties are also available today; these organic canned beans usually contain little or no added salt. Occasionally, frozen varieties of some beans can be found. In addition, you can purchase dried legumes in bags or in bulk and cook them when time permits.

Black Beans (Black Turtle Beans) as the name states are black. They are popular in Caribbean cuisine and also have been eaten in Mexico for over 7,000 years. Use black beans in dips and spreads, soups, salads, chili, stews, burritos, tacos, and more.

Black-eyed Peas (Black-eyed Beans, Cowpeas) are the edible seeds of cowpeas and can be purchased dried, canned, fresh, or frozen. They are thin, oval-shaped, skinned peas which are creamy white with a small black spot on one side. They are popular in the southeastern part of the United States, as well as in other countries such as India and Africa. Use black-eyed peas in soups, casseroles, southern-style dishes, and soul food.

Cannellini Beans (White Kidney Beans) are white and are sold canned. These beans are shaped like human kidneys. They are native to Mexico and Peru and are commonly used in Italian dishes. Cannellini beans can be used to prepare chili, refried beans, stews, casseroles, burgers, salads, and soups.

Chickpeas (Garbanzo Beans, Ceci Beans) are beige and have a round shape. These beans are popular in a wide variety of cuisine including Italian, Middle Eastern, and Indian. Chickpeas can be used to make dips, soups, salads, falafel, burgers, casseroles, stews, and curry dishes.

Fava Beans (Broad Beans, Horse Beans) resemble lima beans but are larger in size. They are green when bought fresh and buff when dried with a dark line running down the ridge where they are split. The Bible refers to this bean and it is native to the Mediterranean region and northern Africa. Fava beans were used in Chinese cuisine over 5,000 years ago and China is still the largest producer of this bean. Use fava beans to prepare dips, salads, soups, stews, and casseroles.

Kidney Beans are brownish/red. They are shaped like human kidneys. They are native to Mexico and Peru and are commonly used in Italian dishes. Kidney beans can be used to prepare chili, refried beans, stews, casseroles, burgers, salads, and soups.

Lima Beans (Baby Limas, Large Butter Beans) are light green. They can be purchased fresh, frozen, canned, or dried. These beans originated in South America. Use lima beans to make spreads, salads, soup, stews, casseroles, and other dishes.

Pinto Beans are a form of the common string bean that has mottled seeds. They are pale pink with brownish flecks. Pinto beans are native to India and are chiefly grown in the southwestern part of the United States. They are popular in Mexican cuisine. Use pinto beans in chili, refried beans, stews, casseroles, and soups.

Red Lentils are really orange-red and cook more quickly then the greenish-brown variety of lentils. They are split in half when dried. They are actually brown lentils with their skins removed. Red lentils are usually imported from the Middle East and turn yellow when cooked. Red lentils can be used to make salads, soups, dal (Indian stews), and other stews.

White Beans (Navy Beans, Great Northern Beans) have a mild flavor and are often used to make baked beans. White beans can be used to prepare a wide variety of dishes including spreads, salads, soups, stews, and casseroles.

Yellow Split Peas are peas that have been shelled, dried, and then split. They are delicious in soups, spreads, dal (Indian stew), and other stews.

MEAT ALTERNATIVES

Today shoppers can choose from over 70 different varieties of vegetarian burgers and dogs. Several of these products are vegan and can be found in natural food stores and in many supermarkets. Veggie burgers and dogs are generally lower in calories and fat than meat-based burgers and hot dogs. Also, meat has no fiber; while most veggie burgers have at least three or four grams of dietary fiber per serving. Beware, however, that veggie burgers are often higher in sodium than ground beef. You can also find many other meat alternatives including soy-based products (such as tofu and tempeh) and wheat-based products (such as gluten or seitan). You can even purchase vegan 'bacon,' vegan 'sausage,' and vegan ground meat.

Vegan 'Bacon' contains no animal ingredients and is sometimes fat-free. This 'bacon' is usually made from soy protein isolate, wheat gluten, and other ingredients. Please note that some vegetarian 'bacons' are not vegan because they contain honey or other non-vegan ingredients. Vegan 'bacon' is sold in the form of Canadian bacon or as bacon bits. It has the texture of bacon and tastes similar to it. You can use this product to replace bacon in any recipe including sandwiches, soups, baked beans, stews, and casseroles.

Chicken-Style Wheat Meat or Gluten is simply seitan or gluten that has the taste and texture of chicken. You can prepare 'chicken' salad, barbecued 'chicken,' stews, stir-fries, and casseroles from this product.

Vegan Ground Meat or Crumbles are made from soy protein and other ingredients. Use 2-2/3 cups of frozen crumbles to replace 1 pound of ground beef which has been browned. The ground 'meat' can be used to make burgers and 'meat' balls. The crumbles are fat-free and excellent to thicken pasta sauces, replace ground meat in Mexican and Italian dishes, to prepare chili, and other dishes.

Vegan 'Hot Dogs' are shaped like meat hot dogs and are usually made from texturized soy protein and other non-meat ingredients. Their texture and flavor are similar to meat hot dogs. Be sure to look for non-fat varieties, too. Use vegan 'hot dogs' in place of meat hot dogs as a sandwich or to prepare stir-fries, stews, or casseroles.

Vegan 'Sausage' comes shaped in small patties or in links. It has the texture and flavor of meat sausages and can be used to prepare any recipe calling for sausage including Italian and other ethnic dishes, stews, casseroles, and stir-fries.

Seitan (Cooked Wheat Gluten, Wheat Meat), pronounced *say-tan*, is wheat gluten that has been simmered and marinated in soy sauce and spices. It is a staple product in China, Korea, Russia, and parts of the Middle East. To prepare seitan, water is added to wheat flour. The mixture is kneaded to a consistency similar to bread dough. The bran and starch are then rinsed repeatedly our of the dough until only the gluten remains. This gluten is then simmered in a broth until it has a meaty texture. Asian grocery stores sell wheat gluten: they call it mien ching or yu mien ching. Seitan can be used to make stews, casseroles, stir-fries, barbecued dishes, and more.

Tempeh, pronounced *tem-pay*, is an ancient staple in Indonesia. It is produced by fermenting presoaked and cooked soybeans. Sometimes a grain is added to the mixture. The soybeans are hulled before being cooked and inoculated with a starter culture grown on hibiscus leaves. The fermentation process binds the beans together and gives them a distinct flavor. Tempeh can be found in natural food stores and some ethnic food markets or supermarkets. It comes in several flavors and varieties and can be fried in a little oil, steamed, boiled, or baked. It can be marinated and grilled and is often served with grains and vegetables. Use tempeh in stews, chili, shish kabobs, casseroles, and burgers.

Tofu is also known as bean curd. It is made from soy milk in a similar fashion to the way cheese is made from cow's milk. The soy milk is heated until it boils, a curdling agent is added, and then the curds are separated from the whey. The curds are then pressed together to form blocks or cubes of tofu. Tofu was produced originally in China about 164 B.C.E., where it is known as dou-fu. In China it is made from a variety of beans and peas. Tofu is now popular in the United States and can be found in the produce section of most supermarkets or in natural food stores, ethnic grocery stores, and gourmet shops. Tofu can be bought in several forms and varieties including firm or extra firm tofu which is wonderful for stir-fries, soups, and stews. Soft or silken tofu is great for dips, dressings, and pies. To make silken tofu, the curds are not pressed at all but are allowed to set with the whey. Silken tofu has a creamier texture than other types of tofu. All varieties are usually sold in cubes and are white. Freeze tofu (after cubing) for at least 48 hours for a chewier texture. Frozen and thawed tofu will turn beige.

MEXICAN PRODUCTS

Look for Mexican products in the ethnic food or gourmet section of your local supermarket or natural foods store. Tortillas are often found fresh in the refrigerator case. Be sure to look for refried beans that do not contain lard. Use these Mexican products to prepare a feast for your family or friends.

Corn Tortillas are the national bread of Mexico. They are made from masa (a paste of water and coarse corn meal), which is rolled out into a flat cake and baked on a griddle. Tortillas can simply be served alone as bread or stuffed with beans and vegetables.

Refried Beans can be purchased premade or made from scratch. Be sure to purchase premade refried beans that do not contain lard!

Salsa is the Spanish and Italian word for sauce. Common salsa ingredients include tomatoes, peppers, onions, salt, vinegar, and garlic. Salsa is sold in many varieties including mild, medium, and hot, as well as chunky or smooth. Serve salsa with raw vegetables or tortilla chips. You can also heat salsa and pour it over cooked vegetables, beans, or grains.

Taco Shells are tortillas that have been fried until crisp and folded into a U-shape. They are native to Mexico. Taco shells can be filled with refried beans, guacamole, chopped tomato, etc.

Tostada Shells are corn tortillas that have been fried until crisp. They are flat and usually topped with refried beans, shredded lettuce, chopped tomato, guacamole, and salsa.

Wheat Tortillas are made from wheat flour and baked on a griddle. They are an unleavened flat bread that originated in Mexico. They can be served simply as bread, stuffed, or layered in casseroles.

MILK AND YOGURT ALTERNATIVES

In this category, it's easier to locate soy and rice beverages than vegan soy yogurt. Many companies now produce alternative milk beverages made from soybeans and/or rice. Some companies also manufacture nut milks, but these are often higher in fat. Vegans may want to purchase soy and/or rice beverages that are fortified. Soy yogurt is presently only manufactured by two companies and is not widely distributed. Your best bet is to look for soy yogurt in a natural foods store.

Soy/Rice Beverages are now found in many supermarkets and natural foods stores and some ethnic groceries. These beverages come in several flavors including plain, vanilla, and carob. Some soy and rice beverages are fortified with vitamin B12, vitamin D, and calcium today. Soymilk is produced during the first step of making tofu. It is actually the liquid coming from soybeans that have been soaked and puréed. Soymilk results if a curdling agent is not added. Soymilk has long been popular in many Asian nations. It first appeared in the United States in the 1920s when it was produced by John Harvey Kellogg. Rice milk is made from partially fermented rice and has a mild flavor. You can also purchase beverages that combine both soy and rice milk. Soy and rice beverages are sold in aseptic packages that do not require refrigeration until opened or in containers similar to those used for selling cow's milk. Some lowfat versions are also available today. Soy and rice beverages can be poured over your favorite breakfast cereal or used to make creamed soups, puddings, and frozen desserts. Soymilk is also used to make soy yogurt.

Soy Yogurt is made from soy milk and an active bacteria culture. It has a yogurt-like taste and comes in various flavors. Beware that some flavors contain honey and are not vegan.

MISCELLANEOUS ITEMS

Here are a some items that you may not be familiar with and are used in a few of the recipes in this book.

Apple Butter is a Pennsylvania-Dutch cooked apple purée dating back until 1765 at least. It's made by cooking and puréeing apples with cider. You can also substitute other fruit butters such as pear butter and peach butter.

Egg Replacer is a combination of powdered starches (primarily potato starch) and leavening agents used to replace eggs in baking. It acts as a binder and is usually sold in a box. To use this egg replacer, it is often necessary to combine it with a liquid. Do not confuse this product with *Egg Beaters* (which is not a vegan product).

Nutritional Yeast (Good Tasting Yeast) is a primary grown dried food yeast grown on a molasses or sugar beet solution. The yeast cells are inactivated by pasteurization and then roller drum dried. Nutritional yeast is considered a "dead" yeast and has no leavening capability. It is yellow in color and comes in a flake or powdered texture. Red Star T-6635+ nutritional yeast has been tested and shown to contain active vitamin B-12. Nutritional yeast has a cheesy taste. It does not taste bitter. Use nutritional yeast as a substitute for Parmesan cheese in many dishes. You can combine it with other ingredients to make sauces and gravies. You can also sprinkle nutritional yeast over popcorn for a delicious snack.

Vegan Mayonnaise looks like non-vegan mayonnaise; however, it does not contain any animal ingredients including eggs and honey. Beware that some vegan mayonnaise products are very high in fat! You may want to purchase a non-fat vegan mayonnaise called *Fat-Free Nayonaise*. Use vegan mayonnaise as a sandwich spread, in dips, or to make salads.

TOMATO PRODUCTS

Be sure to look for organic and/or low-sodium tomato products. Use these products in soups, sauces, stews, and casseroles.

Crushed Tomatoes are simply tomatoes that have been mashed and broken apart. Crushed tomatoes can be used in soups, stews, and casseroles.

Diced Tomatoes are whole tomatoes that have been chopped into small cubes. Diced tomatoes save you time when you need chopped tomatoes in a stew or casserole dish.

Tomato Paste is a very thick concentrate made from cooked tomatoes. It is often used to thicken and flavor sauces. It is also used to make refried beans and can be put in burgers and lentil loaves.

Tomato Purée is made from tomatoes that have been strained and reduced to a thick, yet liquid, consistency. Use tomato purée in sauces.

Tomato Sauce is made out of puréed tomatoes and is often seasoned. It became popular in the United States when Italian immigrants arrived in the late 1800s and early 20th century. Use tomato sauce over pasta, in soups, to make salsa, and much more.

Whole Peeled Tomatoes are tomatoes that have simply had their peels removed. Use whole peeled tomatoes in stews and casserole dishes.

REFERENCE BOOKS
Terrific Information on a Wide Variety of Food

The Book of Food, by Frances Bissell. Henry Holt and Company, New York, NY, 1994.

Companion Guide to Healthy Cooking, by Natalie and Shirley Nigro. Featherstone and Brown, Charlottesville, VA, 1996.

The *Dictionary of American Food and Drink*, by John F. Mariani. Hearst Books, New York, NY, 1994.

A Gourmet's Guide to Dried Fruit and Nuts, by Carole Handslip and Felicity Jackson. HP Books, Los Angeles, CA, 1991.

International Produce Cookbook and Guide, by Marlene Brown. HP Books, Los Angeles, CA, 1989.

The New Foods, by Camille Casumano. Henry Holt and Company, New York, NY, 1989.

The New Professional Chef, edited by Linda Glick Conway. Von Nostrand Reinhold, New York, NY, 1991.

Shopper's Guide to Natural Foods, From the editors of East West Magazine. Avery Publishing Group, Inc., Garden City Park, NY, 1987.

Uncommon Fruits and Vegetables -- A Commonsense Guide, by Elizabeth Schneider. Harper and Row, Publishers, Inc., New York, NY, 1986.

Whole Foods Companion, by Dianne Onstad. Chelsea Green Publishing Company, White River Junction, VT, 1996.

MENU IDEAS

Note: Recipes appearing in this book are in bold.

BREAKFASTS

1) **Yummy French Toast** (pg 160) with maple syrup
   Sliced strawberries, apples, or peaches

2) **Mandarin Pancakes** (pg 160) with maple syrup
   Raisin and nut mixture
   Soothing Orange Juice (pg 155)

3) **Banana Biscuits** (pg 159) with jam or apple butter
   Sautéed potatoes
   Fresh fruit salad

4) **Apple Pockets** (pg 158)
   Strawberry/Banana Shake (pg 156)

5) **Quinoa and Pineapple Cereal** (pg 161)
   or **Amaranth and Peaches** (pg 157)
   Glass of juice

LUNCHES

1) **Bean Burgers** (pg 162) or **Cajun Spiced Tofu Burgers** (pg 136)
   Lettuce and sliced tomato
   Whole grain bun or bread
   Carrot/Date/Peach Salad (pg 48)

2) **Lima Bean Spread** (pg 164) or **Tofu/Pimento Spread** (pg 165)
   Whole grain crackers or raw vegetable sticks
   Pasta Salad (pg 54)
   Glass of juice

3) **Black Bean and Corn Chowder** (pg 40)
   Pita Bread Pizza (pg 164)
   Tossed Greens with Apples and Dates (pg 51)

4) **Spinach/Rice Soup** (pg 47)
   Squash Corn Muffins (pg 163)
   Slice of melon or pineapple

5) **Orange Sweet Potato Soup** (pg 45)
   Chickpea/Apple/Celery Salad (pg 49)
   Lettuce
   Whole Grain Bread

6) **Bean Tacos** (pg 114) or **Quick Black Bean Burritos** (pg 109)
   Rice
   Corn Pudding (pg 169)
   Lemonade

7) Garden salad
   Quick Sloppy Joes (pg 128)
   Whole grain bun or baked white potato
   Glass of Juice

8) **'Hot Dogs,' Peppers, and Onions** (pg 146)
   Whole grain bread
   Potato Salad (pg 57)
   Glass of Juice

9) **Seitan Chili** (pg 122)
   Baked potato or rice
   Fresh fruit

10) **Pasta with Sundried Tomatoes, Garlic, and Spinach** (pg 85)
    or **Spaghetti with Mushroom/Tomato Sauce** (pg 89)
    Garlic bread
    Glass of Juice

11) **Pasta and Bean Soup** (pg 44) or **Barley Bean Soup** (pg 39)
    Seitan/Potato Knishes (pg 151)
    Applesauce

DINNERS

1) **Potato/Carrot Soup** (pg 46)
   Glazed 'Chicken' (pg 121)
   Rice
   Steamed broccoli
   Banana/Oatmeal/Coconut Bar Cookie (pg 166)

2) **Bean Thread Soup** (pg 40)
   Korean-Style Barbecued Seitan (pg 124)
   Lettuce
   Rice or whole grain buns
   Fresh fruit salad

3) **Bulgur/Tofu Loaf** (pg 135)
   Spicy Green Beans (pg 69)
   Mashed potatoes
   Slice of watermelon or other melon

4) **Chickpea Soup** (pg 43)
   Italian Orzo and Tempeh Sauce (pg 127)
   Steamed greens
   Chocolate Pie (pg 168)

5) **Mexican Noodle Casserole** (pg 77)
   Green salad with **Avocado Dressing** (pg 61)
   Slices of mango or papaya

6) **Spicy Mandarin Chickpeas** (pg 110)
   Rice
   Steamed broccoli
   Fresh fruit salad

7) **Quinoa/Sweet Potato Patties** (pg 101)
   Baked Lima Beans (pg 150) or
   Black Bean/Watercress Sauté (pg 118)
   Corn Pudding (pg 169)

8) **Tossed Greens with Apples and Dates** (pg 51)
   Barley Burgers (pg 93) or **Basmati Rice Burgers** (pg 95)
   Mushroom Gravy (pg 90) or **Onions with Barbecue Sauce** (pg 70)
   Corn on the cob
   Glass of Juice

9) **Mandarin/Avocado/Cucumber Salad** (pg 53)
   Unique Lasagna (pg 87) or **Spinach Lasagna** (pg 86)
   Garlic bread

10) **Stuffed Peppers** (pg 149) with **Tomato/Squash Sauce** (pg 92)
    or **Hearty Skillet Dish** (pg 144)
    Penne Salad (pg 56)
    Baked apples

11) **Green Beans and Water Chestnut Salad** (pg 50)
    Chili (pg 111)
    Tortillas or bed of rice
    Pineapple spears

12) **Creamy Carrot and Pasta Soup** (pg 42)
    Bulgur Stuffed Acorn Squash (pg 96)
    Broccoli spears
    Fresh fruit salad

FAT AS A PERCENTAGE OF DAILY VALUE

Fat as a percentage (%) of daily value is a figure being used on food labels. It compares the grams of fat in a food to a total maximum amount of grams of fat that you should be consuming during a day. (Note that this maximum amount is a compromise acceptable to the general population. You may want to aim lower.)

Fat as a percentage of daily value was conceived as a simple way to give the person who knows little or nothing about grams of fat an idea as to whether a food is high or low in fat. There are actually two values on food labels: one for a person who eats 2,000 calories and one for a person who consumes 2,500 calories per day. So, while keeping track of grams of fat is probably the best way to watch your fat intake, the fat as a percentage of daily value can be helpful in determining if a food is high or low in fat.

For this book, we have analyzed the recipes based on the 2,000 calorie figure/65 grams of fat per day. (You may want to eat less fat than that, particularly if you eat fewer calories.) Take our recipe for Barley Bean Soup (pg 39) as an example. It has 6 grams of fat. Based on a 2,000 calories/65 grams of fat per day, it has 9% of the daily value for fat (6 divided by 65 = 9%).

TOP 10 DISHES FOR CALCIUM

How much calcium do we need? The Recommended Daily Allowance (RDA) for adults age 25 and older is 800 milligrams (mg) of calcium per day. An intake of 1,200 milligrams of calcium per day is recommended for those age 11 to 24. In other countries, calcium recommendations are lower than in the United States. For example, British adults are advised to have a calcium intake of 500 milligrams per day.

Tofu Cutlets (240 mg/svg) — Page 140
Sautéed Cabbage and Tempeh with Raisins and Peanuts (199 mg/svg) — Page 125
'Hot Dogs' and Beans Casserole (194 mg/svg) — Page 145
Lasagna Noodle Rollups (194 mg/svg) — Page 75
Tempeh with Lemony Chinese Cabbage (189 mg/svg) — Page 130
Spinach Lasagna (185 mg/svg) — Page 86
Seasoned Tofu over Somen Noodles (176 mg/svg) — Page 139
Tofu and Cruciferous Vegetables (175 mg/svg) — Page 137
Lentil/Spinach Pasta Dish (169 mg/svg) — Page 76
Tofu/Bean Curd/Spinach Sauté (163 mg/svg) —Page 142

TOP 9 DISHES FOR IRON

How much iron do we need? The Recommended Daily Allowance (RDA) for adult men and for post-menopausal women is 10 milligrams of iron per day. Pre-menopausal women are advised to get 15 milligrams of iron per day.

Tofu Cutlets (12 mg/svg) — Page 140
Lentil/Spinach Pasta Dish (11 mg/svg) — Page 76
Layered Noodle Casserole (10 mg/svg) — Page 147
Seasoned Tofu over Somen Noodles (9 mg/svg) — Page 139
Spinach Lasagna (9 mg/svg) — Page 86
'Hot Dogs' and Beans Casserole (8 mg/svg) — Page 145
Lentil/Spinach/Potato Stew (8 mg/svg) — Page 113
Pasta and Apple/Bean Sauce (8 mg/svg) — Page 78
Pasta with Black Bean Sauce (8 mg/svg) — Page 79

SOUPS

BARLEY BEAN SOUP
(Serves 6)

Serve this hearty soup on a chilly evening.

1 cup barley
4 cups water
2 carrots, peeled and finely chopped
1 stalk celery, finely chopped
Small onion, finely chopped
2 teaspoons oil
8 cups vegetable broth
19-ounce can white kidney (cannellini) beans, drained

Bring water to a boil in a medium-size pot. Add barley and reduce heat to medium. Cook covered for 40 minutes.

In a separate large pot, sauté carrots, celery, and onion in oil over medium-high heat for 5 minutes. Add broth, beans, and cooked barley. Heat for 20 minutes longer and serve warm.

Total calories per serving: 233   Fat: 6 grams   Total Fat as % of Daily Value: 9%
Protein: 9 grams   Iron: 2 mg   Carbohydrates: 44 grams   Calcium: 48 mg
Dietary fiber: 9 grams   Sodium: 790 mg

BLACK BEAN AND CORN CHOWDER

(Serves 6)

This simple soup is absolutely delicious.

15-ounce can black beans, rinsed and drained
14-ounce can diced tomatoes or whole tomatoes, chopped
10-ounce box frozen corn kernels
Small onion, finely chopped
2 cups soy milk or other non-dairy milk alternative
4 cups water
1/4 teaspoon garlic powder
Salt and pepper to taste

Heat all the ingredients together in a large pot over medium heat for 25 minutes. Serve warm.

Total calories per serving: 229   Fat: 3 grams   Total Fat as % of Daily Value: 5%
Protein: 11 grams   Iron: 2 mg   Carbohydrates: 34 grams   Calcium: 65 mg
Dietary fiber: 6 grams   Sodium: 299 mg

BEAN THREAD SOUP

(Serves 6)

Enjoy this quick and easy soup.

8 cups vegetable broth
3 carrots (about 1/2 pound), peeled and finely chopped
3 stalks celery, finely chopped
3-3/4-ounce package bean threads (cellophane noodles),
    broken into small pieces

Place broth and vegetables in a large pot and bring to a boil. Reduce heat to medium and cover pot. Cook 10 minutes. Add bean threads and continue to cook covered for 5 minutes. Serve warm.

Total calories per serving: 119   Fat: 4 grams   Total Fat as % of Daily Value: 6%
Protein: 4 grams   Iron: 0.5 mg   Carbohydrates: 27 grams   Calcium: 19 mg
Dietary fiber: 2 grams   Sodium: 625 mg

BULGUR AND TOMATO SOUP
(Serves 6)

Bulgur thickens this soothing soup.

28-ounce can crushed tomatoes or puréed tomatoes
6 cups water or vegetable broth
Small onion, finely chopped
2 stalks celery, finely chopped
1 cup bulgur (about 6 ounces)
1/2 teaspoon oregano
Pepper to taste

Place all the ingredients in a large pot and cook 25 minutes over medium heat. Serve warm in large soup bowls.

Total calories per serving: 221   Fat: 1 gram   Total Fat as % of Daily Value: 2%
Protein: 8 grams   Iron: 2 mg   Carbohydrates: 50 grams   Calcium: 44 mg
Dietary fiber: 14 grams   Sodium: 548 mg

CREAMY CARROT AND PASTA SOUP

(Serves 6)

This is a hearty, yet simple soup to prepare.

6-7 carrots (1 pound), peeled and chopped
8 cups vegetable broth
8 ounces small elbow macaroni
2-1/2 quarts water

Place carrots and broth in a large pot. Bring to a boil, reduce heat, and simmer 15 minutes.

Meanwhile, in a separate pot, cook macaroni in boiling water until tender. Drain.

Purée cooked carrot mixture in blender cup in two batches. Return to pot and add cooked pasta. Reheat and serve.

Total calories per serving: 201   Fat: 4 grams   Total Fat as % of Daily Value: 6%
Protein: 7 grams   Iron: 2 mg   Carbohydrates: 41 grams   Calcium: 27 mg
Dietary fiber: 2 grams   Sodium: 691 mg

CHICKPEA SOUP

(Serves 6-8)

Here's a great substitute for chicken soup and it's easy to prepare.

Two 19-ounce cans chickpeas, rinsed and drained
6-7 carrots (1 pound), peeled and finely chopped
2 large onions, finely chopped
1 Tablespoon oil
Salt and pepper to taste
10 cups water

Sauté chickpeas, carrots, and onions in oil over medium heat in a large pot for 5 minutes. Add seasonings and water. Simmer 30 minutes and serve warm.

Total calories per serving: 228   Fat: 6 grams   Total Fat as % of Daily Value: 9%
Protein: 8 grams   Iron: 3 mg   Carbohydrates: 38 grams   Calcium: 82 mg
Dietary fiber: 12 grams   Sodium: 250 mg

PASTA AND BEAN SOUP

(Serves 8)

Serve this soup as a meal by itself!

8 ounces small elbow macaroni
2-1/2 quarts water
19-ounce can white kidney (cannellini) beans (about 2
     cups pre-cooked), rinsed and drained
10-ounce box frozen chopped spinach
28-ounce can crushed tomatoes
4 cups water
1/2 small onion, finely chopped
1/2 teaspoon garlic powder
Pepper to taste

Bring 2-1/2 quarts water to a boil in a large pot and cook macaroni until
tender (about 8 minutes) and drain.

   Put remaining ingredients in another large pot and cook over medium
heat for 10 minutes. Add cooked pasta, continue cooking another 5
minutes. Serve warm.

Total calories per serving: 208   Fat: 1 gram   Total Fat as % of Daily Value: 2%
Protein: 9 grams   Iron: 4 mg   Carbohydrates: 42 grams   Calcium: 93 mg
Dietary fiber: 6 grams   Sodium: 564 mg

ORANGE SWEET POTATO SOUP

(Serves 6)

Enjoy this sweet soup.

2 pounds sweet potatoes, peeled and cut into 1-inch cubes
4 cups water
1/4 teaspoon cinnamon
Four 10.5-ounce cans mandarin oranges (with liquid)

Place potatoes with water and cinnamon in a large pot. Bring ingredients to a boil. Reduce heat to medium-high, cover pot, and cook 20 minutes. Place half the potato mixture in a blender cup along with half the oranges and purée. Pour into a large pot. Purée the remaining potatoes and oranges and pour this mixture into the pot. Reheat soup for 5 minutes over medium heat before serving.

Total calories per serving: 229   Fat: <1 gram   Total Fat as % of Daily Value: <1%
Protein: 4 grams   Iron: 1 mg   Carbohydrates: 56 grams   Calcium: 64 mg
Dietary fiber: 5 grams   Sodium: 25 mg

POTATO/CARROT SOUP

(Serves 4)

This simple soup tastes great.

1 pound white potatoes, peeled and chopped into small cubes
1/2 pound carrots, peeled and finely chopped
2 cups vegetable broth
3 cups water
1 Tablespoon vegan bacon bits (*Fakin' Bacon Bits*, for example)

Place all the ingredients in a medium-size pot. Bring to a boil. Reduce heat and cook covered over medium heat for 25 minutes. Serve warm.

Total calories per serving: 136   Fat: 2 grams   Total Fat as % of Daily Value: 3%
Protein: 4 grams   Iron: 1 mg   Carbohydrates: 29 grams   Calcium: 23 mg
Dietary fiber: 3 grams   Sodium: 268 mg

SPINACH/RICE SOUP

(Serves 8)

Enjoy this delicious soup.

10-ounce box frozen chopped spinach
1 cup basmati rice
Small onion, finely chopped
1 cup vegetable broth
8 cups water
1/2 teaspoon garlic powder
Pepper to taste
6 ounces plain or lemon soy yogurt (about 3/4 cup)

Place all the ingredients, except the soy yogurt, in a large pot and cook over medium heat for 30 minutes. Add yogurt and cook another 5 minutes. Serve warm.

Total calories per serving: 118   Fat: 1 gram   Total Fat as % of Daily Value: 2%
Protein: 4 grams   Iron: 2 mg   Carbohydrates: 23 grams   Calcium: 65 mg
Dietary fiber: 1 gram   Sodium: 94 mg

SALADS

CARROT/DATE/PEACH SALAD
(Serves 5)

Enjoy this delicious blend of ingredients.

6-7 carrots (1 pound), peeled and grated
4 medium ripe peaches, pitted and finely chopped
5 ounces pitted dates, finely chopped
1/2 teaspoon cinnamon
1/2 cup peach or orange juice

Mix all the ingredients together in a large bowl. Refrigerate at least one hour before serving.

Total calories per serving: 158   Fat: <1 gram   Total Fat as % of Daily Value: <1%
Protein: 2 grams   Iron: 1 mg   Carbohydrates: 40 grams   Calcium: 39 mg
Dietary fiber: 6 grams   Sodium: 33 mg

CHICKPEA/APPLE/CELERY SALAD

(Serves 4)

The mashed chickpeas hold all the ingredients together.

19-ounce can chickpeas — rinsed, drained, and mashed
2 apples — peeled, cored, and finely chopped
1 stalk celery, finely chopped
1/4 teaspoon cinnamon

Mix all the ingredients together in a medium-size bowl. Chill before serving on a bed of lettuce or as a sandwich spread on bread.

Total calories per serving: 158   Fat: 3 grams   Total Fat as % of Daily Value: 5%
Protein: 5 grams   Iron: 2 mg   Carbohydrates: 30 grams   Calcium: 46 mg
Dietary fiber: 8 grams   Sodium: 289 mg

MARINATED CHICKPEA AND SNOW PEA SALAD

(Serves 4)

This is a very pretty salad.

19-ounce can chickpeas, drained and rinsed
1/4 pound snow peas, finely chopped with ends snipped off
1/2 small red onion, finely chopped
1 cup fat-free vegan Italian dressing

Steam snow peas for 5 minutes. Mix all the ingredients together in a medium-size bowl. Refrigerate at least 1 hour before serving chilled.

Total calories per serving: 166   Fat: 3 grams   Total Fat as % of Daily Value: 5%
Protein: 6 grams   Iron: 2 mg   Carbohydrates: 27 grams   Calcium: 54 mg
Dietary fiber: 8 grams   Sodium: 840 mg

GREEN BEANS AND WATER CHESTNUT SALAD
(Serves 4)

Water chestnuts add a nice crunch to this salad.

1 pound green beans, rinsed and chopped into bite-size
    pieces with ends snipped off
8-ounce can sliced water chestnuts, drained and chopped
    into halves
1 teaspoon oregano
1/3 cup fat-free vegan Italian dressing

Steam green beans over boiling water in a large pot for 5 minutes.
Remove from heat.

Combine ingredients in a medium-size bowl. Refrigerate at least one
hour before serving chilled.

Total calories per serving: 75   Fat: <1 gram   Total Fat as % of Daily Value: <1%
Protein: 3 grams   Iron: 2 mg   Carbohydrates: 17 grams   Calcium: 45 mg
Dietary fiber: 2 grams   Sodium: 221 mg

TOSSED GREENS WITH APPLES AND DATES

(Serves 6)

Be sure to experiment with different salad greens.
You can also substitute chopped figs for the dates.

1/2 pound green leaf lettuce, rinsed and torn into bite-size
  pieces
1/2 pound romaine lettuce or other salad greens, rinsed and
  torn into bite-size pieces
3 apples, peeled, cored, and chopped
1 cup chopped pitted dates (about 5 ounces)
2/3 cup apple juice
1/2 teaspoon cinnamon

Toss all the ingredients together in a large bowl and serve.

Total calories per serving: 142   Fat: 1 gram   Total Fat as % of Daily Value: 2%
Protein: 2 grams   Iron: 1 mg   Carbohydrates: 36 grams   Calcium: 39 mg
Dietary fiber: 5 grams   Sodium: 8 mg

LENTIL FRUIT SALAD
(Serves 6)

This salad can be served as a meal in itself.

1-1/2 cups lentils
5 cups water
2 apples — cored, peeled, and finely chopped
2 pears, cored and finely chopped
2 bananas, peeled and thinly sliced
1/4 cup orange or apple juice

Cook lentils in water in a medium-size pot over medium heat for 55 minutes. Drain off any excess liquid and allow lentils to cool.

Place lentils in a medium-size bowl. Add remaining ingredients and stir well. Cover and refrigerate for at least 2 hours before serving chilled.

Total calories per serving: 227   Fat: 1 gram   Total Fat as % of Daily Value: 2%
Protein: 11 grams   Iron: 4 mg   Carbohydrates: 47 grams   Calcium: 32 mg
Dietary fiber: 8 grams   Sodium: 3 mg

MANDARIN ORANGE/AVOCADO/ CUCUMBER SALAD

(Serves 8)

Mandarin oranges take the place of dressing in this delicious salad.

1 pound romaine lettuce, rinsed and cut into bite-size
   pieces
2 cucumbers, peeled and chopped
Three 10.5-ounce cans mandarin oranges, drained
Small ripe avocado — peeled, pit removed, and chopped

Toss all the ingredients together in a large bowl. Refrigerate at least 1/2 hour and serve chilled.

Total calories per serving: 90   Fat: 3 grams   Total Fat as % of Daily Value: 5%
Protein: 2 grams   Iron: 1 mg   Carbohydrates: 15 grams   Calcium: 46 mg
Dietary fiber: 2 grams   Sodium: 14 mg

MEXICAN TOSSED SALAD
(Serves 6)

Enjoy this creative hearty salad!

1 pound green leaf or romaine lettuce, rinsed and cut into
  bite-size pieces
14-ounce can pinto beans, rinsed and drained
Small ripe avocado, pit removed, peeled, and chopped
1 cup salsa

Toss all the ingredients together in a large salad bowl. Chill for at least
1/2 hour and serve cold.

Total calories per serving: 112   Fat: 4 grams   Total Fat as % of Daily Value: 6%
Protein: 5 grams   Iron: 2 mg   Carbohydrates: 15 grams   Calcium: 84 mg
Dietary fiber: 2 grams   Sodium: 466 mg

PASTA SALAD
(Serves 5)

Enjoy this colorful salad.

1 pound pasta (elbows, rotini, for example), cooked
10-ounce box frozen corn kernels, precooked
7-ounce jar roasted peppers, drained and finely chopped
3-ounce jar capers, drained
3/4 cup vegan fat-free Italian dressing

Toss the ingredients together in a large bowl and refrigerate at least one
hour before serving.

Total calories per serving: 402   Fat: 2 grams   Total Fat as % of Daily Value: 3%
Protein: 14 grams   Iron: 5 mg   Carbohydrates: 71 grams   Calcium: 16 mg
Dietary fiber: 4 grams   Sodium: 1058 mg

PASTA AND KIDNEY BEAN SALAD

(Serves 5)

Here's a slightly spicy salad you'll enjoy.

1/2 pound pasta (elbows, rotini, for example)
2-1/2 quarts water
15-1/2-ounce can kidney beans, rinsed and drained
2 medium carrots, peeled and grated
2 stalks celery, chopped
3 Tablespoons hot cherry peppers

Cook pasta in boiling water until tender. Drain.

Stir all ingredients together in a large bowl. Chill in refrigerator before serving.

Total calories per serving: 257   Fat: 1 gram   Total Fat as % of Daily Value: 2%
Protein: 11 grams   Iron: 3 mg   Carbohydrates: 51 grams   Calcium: 46 mg
Dietary fiber: 6 grams   Sodium: 187 mg

PENNE SALAD
(Serves 8)

*Penne is a type of pasta found in many supermarkets
and Italian or gourmet shops. This is a hearty salad!*

1 pound penne
5 quarts water
1 cup peeled and sliced carrots, steamed
2 cups broccoli florets, steamed
2 medium ripe tomatoes, chopped
1 Tablespoon fresh basil, finely minced
2/3 cup fat-free vegan Italian dressing

Precook pasta in boiling water until tender and drain. Stir the ingredients
together in a large bowl. Chill at least 30 minutes. Toss before serving.

Total calories per serving: 241   Fat: 1 gram   Total Fat as % of Daily Value: 2%
Protein: 8 grams   Iron: 3 mg   Carbohydrates: 48 grams   Calcium: 29 mg
Dietary fiber: 2 grams   Sodium: 200 mg

POTATO SALAD

(Serves 5)

This salad is terrific for picnics!

2-1/2 pounds white potatoes, peeled and chopped into bite-
  size pieces
1 gallon water
1 large cucumber, peeled and finely chopped
2 large carrots, peeled and finely chopped
1/4 cup fresh dill, minced or 1 Tablespoon dried dill
1/4 cup vegan mayonnaise (*Nayonaise*, for example)

Cook potatoes in boiling water in a large pot until tender. Drain and
place in a large bowl. Add remaining ingredients. Toss well and
refrigerate at least one hour. Toss again before serving.

Total calories per serving: 233   Fat: 3 grams   Total Fat as % of Daily Value: 5%
Protein: 6 grams   Iron: 2 mg   Carbohydrates: 47 grams   Calcium: 37 mg
Dietary fiber: 4 grams   Sodium: 112 mg

POTATO AND BEAN SALAD

(Serves 6)

This salad is a meal by itself.

2 pounds white potatoes, peeled and chopped into bite-size
    pieces
19-ounce can white kidney (cannellini) beans, rinsed and
    drained
10-ounce bag frozen and thawed or 15-ounce can (drained),
    baby lima beans
2 stalks celery, finely chopped
1 Tablespoon fresh dill weed or 1 teaspoon dried dill weed
1/2 cup fat-free vegan Italian dressing

Cook potatoes in boiling water in large pot until tender (about 15
minutes) and drain. Allow potatoes to cool.

   Mix remaining ingredients together in a large bowl. Add cooked
potatoes, stir well, and refrigerate at least 1/2 hour before serving.

Total calories per serving: 248   Fat: 1 gram   Total Fat as % of Daily Value: 2%
Protein: 10 grams   Iron: 3 mg   Carbohydrates: 50 grams   Calcium: 55 mg
Dietary fiber: 9 grams   Sodium: 354 mg

RICE SALAD

(Serves 6)

Basmati rice is popular in Indian cuisine and similar American grown brands are packaged under the names of Texmati, Kasmati, and Calmati.

14-ounce box basmati rice (2 cups)
4 cups water
3 stalks celery, chopped
2 apples — peeled, cored, and chopped
1 cup pitted dried prunes (about 6 ounces), chopped
1 cup fat-free vegan Italian dressing

Place rice and water in a medium-size pot and bring to a boil. Reduce heat, cover, and simmer for 20 minutes. Remove from stove and allow to sit 5 more minutes uncovered.

When rice is done, add the remaining ingredients. Chill for 1 hour before serving.

Total calories per serving: 353   Fat: 1 gram   Total Fat as % of Daily Value: 2%
Protein: 6 grams   Iron: 4 mg   Carbohydrates: 79 grams   Calcium: 42 mg
Dietary fiber: 4 grams   Sodium: 395 mg

WHITE BEAN SALAD

(Serves 4)

Great northern, navy, and/or cannellini beans
are great in this hearty salad.

Two 14-ounce cans white beans (about 3 cups cooked),
    rinsed and drained
2 medium ripe tomatoes, finely chopped
2 Tablespoons fresh basil, finely chopped
1/4 cup vegetable broth
2 Tablespoons lemon juice

Mix all the ingredients together in a medium-size bowl. Refrigerate at
least one hour before serving chilled.

Total calories per serving: 165   Fat: 1 gram   Total Fat as % of Daily Value: 2%
Protein: 8 grams   Iron: 3 mg   Carbohydrates: 30 grams   Calcium: 66 mg
Dietary fiber: 8 grams   Sodium: 440 mg

DRESSINGS

AVOCADO DRESSING

(Makes about 2 cups -- 16 servings)

This dressing will keep refrigerated for up to one week.
Serve over your favorite green salad.

1 small avocado, peeled and pit removed
2 cucumbers — peeled, sliced lengthwise, and seeds
   removed
Salt and pepper to taste

Place all the ingredients in a food processor cup. Purée and chill before
serving.

Total calories per 2 TB serving: 20   Fat: 1 gram   Total Fat as % of Daily Value: 2%
Protein: <1 gram   Iron: <1 mg   Carbohydrates: 2 grams   Calcium: 6 mg
Dietary fiber: <1 gram   Sodium: 2 mg

CITRUS FRUIT DRESSING

(Makes about 2-1/4 cups -- 18 servings)

Enjoy this creamy unique salad dressing.

10.5-ounce package lite tofu
1 Tablespoon maple syrup
1/4 cup orange juice
1/4 teaspoon dried mint
1 cup citrus fruit (mandarin oranges, oranges, grapefruits, etc.), seeds removed and chopped

Place the tofu, syrup, juice, and mint in a food processor cup. Blend until creamy. Stir in chopped fruit, mixing well, then chill before serving.

Total calories per 2 TB serving: 16   Fat: <1 gram   Total Fat as % of Daily Value: <1%
Protein: 1 gram   Iron: <1 mg   Carbohydrates: 2 grams   Calcium: 5 mg
Dietary fiber: <1 grams   Sodium: 14 mg

CUCUMBER DRESSING

(Makes about 2 cups -- 16 servings)

This dressing will keep refrigerated for up to one week.

Small cucumber, peeled
1 Tablespoon cider vinegar
1 cup plain soy yogurt
2 teaspoons fresh dill, finely minced or 1 teaspoon dried dill weed

Place the ingredients in a food processor cup and purée. Chill and serve.

Total calories per 2 TB serving: 14   Fat: <1 gram   Total Fat as % of Daily Value: <1%
Protein: 1 gram   Iron: 0 mg   Carbohydrates: 2 grams   Calcium: 5 mg
Dietary fiber: <1 gram   Sodium: 4 mg

MANGO DRESSING

(Makes about 1-1/4 cups -- 10 servings)

This is an absolutely delicious dressing.
Serve over your favorite salad or as a dip for raw vegetables.

1 ripe mango — peeled, pit removed, and chopped
6 ounces vanilla soy yogurt

Place both ingredients in a food processor cup. Blend until creamy and chill before serving.

Total calories per 2 TB serving: 28   Fat: <1 gram   Total Fat as % of Daily Value: <1%
Protein: <1 gram   Iron: <1 mg   Carbohydrates: 5 grams   Calcium: 3 mg
Dietary fiber: <1 gram   Sodium: 3 mg

SWEET TOMATO DRESSING

(Makes about 2 cups -- 16 servings)

Enjoy this quick and easy salad dressing.

8-ounce can tomato sauce
1/4 cup molasses
1 medium ripe tomato, finely chopped
1/2 cucumber, peeled and finely chopped
1/4 teaspoon oregano

Place all the ingredients in a bowl and mix well. Chill before serving.

Total calories per 2 TB serving: 19   Fat: <1 gram   Total Fat as % of Daily Value: <1%
Protein: <1 gram   Iron: <1 mg   Carbohydrates: 5 grams   Calcium: 19 mg
Dietary fiber: <1 gram   Sodium: 89 mg

VEGETABLES

BAKED ACORN SQUASH WITH WHOLE GRAIN BREAD CRUMBS AND APPLES

(Serves 8)

Here's a delicious autumn dish.

2 pounds acorn squash — peeled, sliced in half, and seeds removed
1 cup apple juice
3 ounces dried prunes, chopped
2 apples — cored, peeled, and chopped
4-5 slices whole grain bread, chopped in 1-inch cubes
1/4 teaspoon cinnamon
2 Tablespoons vegan margarine

Preheat oven to 375 degrees. Meanwhile, slice acorn squash into 1/3-inch thick slices. Place sliced squash in a non-stick 13"x9"x2" baking pan. Pour apple juice over squash in pan.

Mix prunes, apples, and bread cubes together. Layer on top of squash. Sprinkle with cinnamon and place dots of margarine on top. Bake 30 minutes. Serve warm.

Total calories per serving: 160   Fat: 4 grams   Total Fat as % of Daily Value: 6%
Protein: 3 grams   Iron: 1 mg   Carbohydrates: 32 grams   Calcium: 54 mg
Dietary fiber: 1 grams   Sodium: 118 mg

APPLES AND LIMA BEANS

(Serves 4)

This unique combination tastes wonderful.

10-ounce package frozen lima beans
3 apples — peeled, cored, and chopped
Small onion, finely chopped
1 cup water
1/2 teaspoon cinnamon
1/4 teaspoon nutmeg

Heat all the ingredients in a covered medium-size pot over medium-high heat for 10 minutes. Uncover pot and continue to cook 10 minutes longer. Serve warm.

Total calories per serving: 133   Fat: 1 gram   Total Fat as % of Daily Value: 2%
Protein: 5 grams   Iron: 1 mg   Carbohydrates: 29 grams   Calcium: 23 mg
Dietary fiber: 5 grams   Sodium: 38 mg

ASPARAGUS WITH DRIED FRUIT

(Serves 3)

This is a beautiful unique side dish.

1/3 pound thin asparagus, chopped
1 cup dried fruit (different varieties), finely chopped
1/2 cup water
5-1/2 ounces prune juice (small can)

Place all the ingredients in a medium-size pot and cook over medium heat for 15 minutes. Serve warm.

Total calories per serving: 181   Fat: 1 gram   Total Fat as % of Daily Value: 2%
Protein: 3 grams   Iron: 2 mg   Carbohydrates: 45 grams   Calcium: 30 mg
Dietary fiber: 4 grams   Sodium: 12 mg

TOSSED GREENS AND BEANS

(Serves 4)

Serve this hearty side dish and you're sure to get rave reviews.

19-ounce can cooked beans (white or red kidney beans,
    for example), rinsed and drained
1/2 cup vegetable broth
Small onion, finely chopped
4 cups kale or collard greens, finely chopped
2 medium ripe tomatoes, chopped
1 teaspoon cumin

Sauté ingredients over medium-high heat for 10 minutes in a large pot. Serve warm.

Total calories per serving: 142   Fat: 1 gram   Total Fat as % of Daily Value: 2%
Protein: 9 grams   Iron: 2 mg   Carbohydrates: 27 grams   Calcium: 67 mg
Dietary fiber: 9 grams   Sodium: 536 mg

SAUTÉED BRUSSELS SPROUTS

(Serves 3)

Here's a simple dish your guests will enjoy.

1/2 pound Brussels sprouts, ends chopped off
2 teaspoons oil
1 Tablespoon vegan 'bacon' bits

Slice Brussels sprouts in half lengthwise then sauté them in oil in a
medium-size non-stick frying pan over medium-high heat for 10 minutes.
Add 'bacon' bits and sauté 5 minutes longer. Serve warm.

Total calories per serving: 71   Fat: 4 grams   Total Fat as % of Daily Value: 6%
Protein: 4 grams   Iron: 1 mg   Carbohydrates: 8 grams   Calcium: 32 mg
Dietary fiber: 3 grams   Sodium: 44 mg

SAUTÉED CABBAGE/CORN

(Serves 5)

Enjoy this delicious dish.

6-ounce package vegan 'bacon,' chopped into small pieces
Small green cabbage (1-1/2 pounds), cored and chopped
10-ounce box frozen corn
3 Tablespoons vegetable broth

In a non-stick, lightly oiled, large frying pan, fry 'bacon' pieces over a
medium-high heat for 8 minutes, until crisp on both sides. Add cabbage,
corn, and broth and sauté 7 minutes over medium heat. Serve warm.

Total calories per serving: 146   Fat: 4 grams   Total Fat as % of Daily Value: 6%
Protein: 9 grams   Iron: 1 mg   Carbohydrates: 12 grams   Calcium: 120 mg
Dietary fiber: 2 grams   Sodium: 181 mg

CAULIFLOWER CURRY
(Serves 4)

Serve small portions of this dish with at least 1 cup of rice per person.

Large head cauliflower
1 cup lite coconut milk
1/2 cup water
1 teaspoon curry powder
Pinch cayenne
2 teaspoons cornstarch

Chop cauliflower into bite-size pieces. Cover with water in a pot and bring to a boil. Reduce heat and simmer 15 minutes until tender.

Stir coconut milk, water, curry powder, cayenne, and cornstarch constantly with a whisk in a small pot over medium-high heat. Bring to a boil to thicken. Turn off heat.

Mix sauce with cooked cauliflower and serve over rice.

Total calories per serving: 104   Fat: 6 grams   Total Fat as % of Daily Value: 9%
Protein: 6 grams   Iron: 2 mg   Carbohydrates: 10 grams   Calcium: 78 mg
Dietary fiber: 7 grams   Sodium: 97 mg

SPICY GREEN BEANS

(Serves 5)

This simple dish tastes terrific! Cold leftovers are also good.

2 pounds fresh green beans, ends snapped off
2 cups (15.5-ounce jar) salsa

Cook green beans in water for 15 minutes and drain.

Place salsa in small pot and simmer for 3 minutes. Pour warm salsa over cooked green beans. Serve warm.

Total calories per serving: 72   Fat: <1 gram   Total Fat as % of Daily Value: <1%
Protein: 4 grams   Iron: 2 mg   Carbohydrates: 16 grams   Calcium: 80 mg
Dietary fiber: 5 grams   Sodium: 727 mg

GREENS, BEETS, AND PEACHES

(Serves 5)

This creative dish is quite pleasing to the eye.

1 pound kale, rinsed and chopped into bite-size pieces
15-ounce can beets, drained and chopped into 1-inch cubes
or 2 cups cooked fresh beets, chopped
16-ounce can juice-pack peaches, drained and chopped into
1-inch cubes or 2 cups fresh peaches, chopped

Sauté ingredients in a large deep pot over medium heat for 8 minutes. Serve warm.

Total calories per serving: 79   Fat: <1 gram   Total Fat as % of Daily Value: <1%
Protein: 2 grams   Iron: 2 mg   Carbohydrates: 19 grams   Calcium: 39 mg
Dietary fiber: 3 grams   Sodium: 281 mg

SEASONED OKRA, TOMATOES, AND WATER CHESTNUTS

(Serves 4)

This is a flavorful and unique side dish.

3/4 pound fresh okra, chopped in half and ends removed
2 medium ripe tomatoes, chopped
8-ounce can water chestnuts, drained
1/4 cup vegetable broth
1/4 teaspoon curry powder
1/4 teaspoon coriander
1/4 teaspoon cumin
Salt and pepper to taste

Cook all the ingredients together in a medium-size pot over medium heat for 15 minutes, stirring occasionally to prevent sticking. Serve warm.

Total calories per serving: 58   Fat: <1 gram   Total Fat as % of Daily Value: <1%
Protein: 2 grams   Iron: 1 mg   Carbohydrates: 13 grams   Calcium: 58 mg
Dietary fiber: 2 grams   Sodium: 27 mg

ONIONS WITH BARBECUE SAUCE

(Serves 4)

Serve this dish over your favorite veggie burger or as a side dish.

2 medium onions, sliced into rings
1/4 cup vegetable broth
1/2 cup vegan barbecue sauce

Sauté onions in broth in a large pan over medium-high heat for 8 minutes. Add barbecue sauce and heat 2 minutes longer. Serve warm.

Total calories per serving: 65   Fat: 1 gram   Total Fat as % of Daily Value: 2%
Protein: 1 gram   Iron: <1 mg   Carbohydrates: 14 grams   Calcium: 10 mg
Dietary fiber: 1 gram   Sodium: 490 mg

SAUTÉED PORTABELLO MUSHROOMS
(Serves 3)

This mushroom dish is absolutely delicious!

6 ounces sliced portabello mushrooms
1 teaspoon olive oil
1 teaspoon nutritional yeast
1 teaspoon fresh dill weed, finely chopped or 1/4 teaspoon
   dried dill weed
2 teaspoons red wine vinegar

Sauté mushrooms in oil over medium heat in a large frying pan for 3
minutes. Sprinkle on the remaining ingredients and sauté 3 minutes
longer. Serve warm.

Total calories per serving: 28   Fat: 2 grams   Total Fat as % of Daily Value: 3%
Protein: 1 gram   Iron: 1 mg   Carbohydrates: 3 grams   Calcium: 3 mg
Dietary fiber: 1 gram   Sodium: 2 mg

POTATO/APPLE/ SAUERKRAUT DISH

(Serves 5)

Savor this unique combination.

6 cups water
1-1/2 pounds white potatoes, peeled and chopped
3 apples — peeled, cored, and chopped
1 cup sauerkraut, drained
1 teaspoon caraway seeds
1/4 cup water

Cook potatoes in 6 cups water over medium-high heat until tender (about 20 minutes). Drain.

Place cooked potatoes and remaining ingredients in a medium-size pot. Simmer over medium heat for 8 minutes. Serve warm.

Total calories per serving: 110   Fat: <1 gram   Total Fat as % of Daily Value: <1%
Protein: 2 grams   Iron: 1 mg   Carbohydrates: 26 grams   Calcium: 22 mg
Dietary fiber: 3 grams   Sodium: 316 mg

TOSSED POTATOES, PEAS, AND TOMATOES

(Serves 5)

Enjoy these vegetables served with dill weed.

2-1/2 pounds white potatoes, peeled and chopped into
    1-inch cubes
5 cups water
10-ounce box frozen peas
1-1/2 cups ripe tomatoes, finely chopped or 14.5-ounce can
    whole tomatoes, chopped
1 Tablespoon fresh dill weed, finely chopped or 1 teaspoon
    dried dill weed
Salt and pepper to taste

Cook the white potatoes in the water in a large pot over medium-high heat for 20 minutes. Drain potatoes.

Sauté cooked potatoes with remaining ingredients over medium heat for 5 minutes. Serve warm.

Total calories per serving: 239   Fat: 1 gram   Total Fat as % of Daily Value: 2%
Protein: 8 grams   Iron: 3 mg   Carbohydrates: 52 grams   Calcium: 33 mg
Dietary fiber: 7 grams   Sodium: 70 mg

THAI YELLOW VEGETABLE CURRY
(Serves 3)

This spicy dish calls for Thai yellow curry paste which can be found in gourmet and natural foods stores.
Make sure the paste does not contain fish sauce.

1 cup vegetable broth
1/3 cup plain soy milk
1 to 2 teaspoons vegan Thai yellow curry paste (*Thai Kitchen* variety, for example)
1 Tablespoon cornstarch
1 pound zucchini, sliced
2 carrots, peeled and sliced
1/4 medium onion, finely chopped
2 Tablespoons vegetable broth

In a small pot over high heat bring 1 cup vegetable broth, soy milk, curry paste, and corn starch to a boil. Stir constantly with a whisk until mixture thickens. Remove from heat.

In separate large frying pan, sauté vegetables in 2 Tablespoons broth for 5 minutes over medium-high heat.

Serve vegetables with curry sauce over cooked rice or pasta.

Total calories per serving: 84   Fat: 2 grams   Total Fat as % of Daily Value: 3%
Protein: 3 grams   Iron: 3 mg   Carbohydrates: 16 grams   Calcium: 52 mg
Dietary fiber: 3 grams   Sodium: 101 mg

PASTA

LASAGNA NOODLE ROLLUPS

(Serves 6)

This dish looks terrific and is easy to serve at a party.

10-ounce box lasagna noodles (about 12 noodles)
4 quarts water
Two 10-ounce boxes frozen chopped spinach
3 cups tomato sauce
Two 15-ounce cans kidney or pinto beans — rinsed,
    drained, and mashed

Bring the water to a boil in a large pot and add the lasagna noodles a few at a time. Cook noodles for about 10 minutes or until tender. Drain.

Meanwhile, in a separate small pot, cook the spinach per instructions on the package. Drain off any excess liquid.

Preheat oven to 375 degrees. Place a thin layer of tomato sauce in the bottom of a 13" x 9" x 2" baking pan and set aside. Carefully place one cooked lasagna noodle at a time on a clean surface. Spread 1/12th of the mashed beans on the noodle, followed by 1/12th of the cooked spinach. Next, slowly roll up the noodle and place it with the end of the roll face down in the baking pan. Repeat with the remaining noodles and other ingredients.

Cover the rollups with the remaining sauce and bake for 15 minutes at 375 degrees. Serve 2 warm rollups per person.

Total calories per serving: 419   Fat: 2 grams   Total Fat as % of Daily Value: 3%
Protein: 19 grams   Iron: 7 mg   Carbohydrates: 84 grams   Calcium: 194 mg
Dietary fiber: 11 grams   Sodium: 1155 mg

LENTIL/SPINACH PASTA DISH
(Serves 4)

A hearty lentil-based sauce is served over your favorite choice of pasta.

1 pound pasta, cooked and drained
2 cups cooked lentils or 1 cup dried lentils cooked in 2-1/2
    cups water
10-ounce box frozen chopped spinach, cooked and drained
2/3 cup raisins
15-ounce can tomato sauce
1/2 teaspoon cinnamon

Simmer all the ingredients except the pasta over low heat for 10 minutes.
Pour sauce over cooked pasta and serve warm.

Total calories per serving: 659   Fat: 3 grams   Total Fat as % of Daily Value: 5%
Protein: 28 grams   Iron: 11 mg   Carbohydrates: 135 grams   Calcium: 169 mg
Dietary fiber: 12 grams   Sodium: 717 mg

MEXICAN NOODLE CASSEROLE

(Serves 8)

Enjoy this layered casserole dish.

1 pound lasagna noodles
5 quarts water
Two 16-ounce cans vegan refried beans
Two 16-ounce jars salsa
2 small ripe avocados, pits removed
1 Tablespoon lemon juice

Cook lasagna noodles in boiling water in a large pot for 10 minutes. Drain noodles.

Meanwhile, preheat oven to 375 degrees. In a 13"x9"x2" pan spread ingredients to form the following layers: 1/4 cooked noodles; 1 can refried beans; 1/4 cooked noodles; 1 jar salsa; 1/4 cooked noodles; 1 can refried beans; 1/4 cooked noodles; and 1 jar salsa. Bake layered casserole at 375 degrees for 25 minutes.

While the casserole is baking, mash the ripe avocado with the lemon juice until smooth. When casserole is done remove from oven. Spread mashed avocado mixture on top of casserole just before serving.

Total calories per serving: 414   Fat: 8 grams   Total Fat as % of Daily Value: 12%
Protein: 17 grams   Iron: 6 mg   Carbohydrates: 72 grams   Calcium: 94 mg
Dietary fiber: 10 grams   Sodium: 1448 mg

PASTA AND APPLE/BEAN SAUCE
(Serves 4)

This is a hearty dish.

1 pound pasta, cooked
3 apples — peeled, cored, and chopped
Two 15-ounce cans beans (chickpeas, kidney, and pinto, for
    example), rinsed and drained
Small onion, finely chopped
1/4 teaspoon nutmeg

Heat apples, beans, onion, and nutmeg together in a medium-size pot over medium heat for 10 minutes. Stir often. Serve warm over the cooked pasta.

Total calories per serving: 653   Fat: 3 grams   Total Fat as % of Daily Value: 5%
Protein: 26 grams   Iron: 8 mg   Carbohydrates: 132 grams   Calcium: 85 mg
Dietary fiber: 16 grams   Sodium: 746 mg

PASTA WITH
BLACK BEAN SAUCE

(Serves 4)

Enjoy this delicious sauce.

1 pound pasta, cooked
15-ounce can black beans, rinsed and drained
10.5-ounce can mandarin oranges, drained
2 large ripe tomatoes, finely chopped
1/2 teaspoon cinnamon

Heat beans, oranges, tomatoes, and cinnamon in a medium-size pot over medium heat for 8 minutes. Stir occasionally. Serve over the cooked pasta.

Total calories per serving: 603   Fat: 3 grams   Total Fat as % of Daily Value: 5%
Protein: 25 grams   Iron: 8 mg   Carbohydrates: 121 grams   Calcium: 61 mg
Dietary fiber: 8 grams   Sodium: 319 mg

PASTA WITH GRATED VEGETABLES AND CARROT/RAISIN SAUCE

(Serves 6)

Enjoy this creative pasta dish.

1 pound pasta of your choice (elbows, for example)
5 quarts water
6-7 carrots (1 pound), peeled and chopped
1-1/2 cups raisins (about 8 ounces)
1 cup water
Small head green cabbage (about 1-1/4 pounds), cored and grated
2 medium zucchini, grated
1 large red bell pepper — cored, seeds removed, and grated

Cook pasta in 5 quarts of boiling water in a large pot until tender. Drain.

At the same time, cook the carrots and raisins in 1 cup of water in a medium-size pot over medium-high heat for 10 minutes. Pour cooked carrots and raisins into a food processor bowl and blend for 3 minutes.

Toss cooked pasta and grated vegetables together. Pour sauce over the mixture and serve immediately.

Total calories per serving: 460   Fat: 2 grams   Total Fat as % of Daily Value: 3%
Protein: 14 grams   Iron: 5 mg   Carbohydrates: 101 grams   Calcium: 110 mg
Dietary fiber: 4 grams   Sodium: 55 mg

PASTA WITH LIMA BEAN AND CORN SAUCE

(Serves 5)

Here's a quick and easy pasta dish.

1 pound pasta of your choice
5 quarts water
10-ounce box frozen baby lima beans
10-ounce box frozen corn kernels
1-1/2 cups water
2 Tablespoons oil
1/2 cup nutritional yeast
1/4 cup unbleached white flour
2 teaspoons tamari or soy sauce
1 cup vegetable broth

Cook pasta in boiling water in a large pot for 8-10 minutes until tender. Drain.

Meanwhile, cook lima beans and corn in 1-1/2 cups water in a medium-size pot over medium-high heat for 10 minutes. Drain.

In a small pot, heat oil over medium-high heat. Stir in the yeast and flour using a whisk for 1 minute. Add the tamari or soy sauce and vegetable broth. Stir sauce until it thickens.

Mix sauce and cooked vegetables together and serve over cooked pasta.

Total calories per serving: 527 Fat: 8 grams Total Fat as % of Daily Value: 12%
Protein: 18 grams Iron: 6 mg Carbohydrates: 85 grams Calcium: 34 mg
Dietary fiber: 8 grams Sodium: 368 mg

PASTA WITH ONION SAUCE
(Serves 5)

This is a simple, yet delicious, pasta dish.

1 pound pasta of your choice
5 quarts water
3 large onions, peeled and sliced into thin rings
1 Tablespoon tarragon
1 Tablespoon oil
1 cup vegetable broth

Cook pasta in boiling water in a large pot for 8-10 minutes until tender. Drain.

Meanwhile, in a separate large non-stick pot, sauté onions and tarragon in oil over medium-high heat for 10 minutes. Add vegetable broth and continue to cook 5 minutes longer. Serve onion sauce over the cooked pasta.

Total calories per serving: 402   Fat: 5 grams   Total Fat as % of Daily Value: 8%
Protein: 13 grams   Iron: 4 mg   Carbohydrates: 75 grams   Calcium: 31 mg
Dietary fiber: 3 grams   Sodium: 217 mg

PASTA AND SAVOY CABBAGE
(Serves 5)

Here's a quick and easy pasta dish.

1 pound pasta of your choice
5 quarts water
1 pound Savoy cabbage, shredded
2 cups vegetable broth

Cook pasta in boiling water in a large pot for 8-10 minutes. Drain.

In a separate large pot, sauté the cabbage in the vegetable broth for 10 minutes. Mix the sautéed cabbage and cooked pasta together and serve warm.

Total calories per serving: 368   Fat: 2 grams   Total Fat as % of Daily Value: 3%
Protein: 14 grams   Iron: 5 mg   Carbohydrates: 74 grams   Calcium: 49 mg
Dietary fiber: 4 grams   Sodium: 120 mg

PASTA AND
TOMATO/PEACH SAUCE
(Serves 4)

With a simple, yet unique sauce pasta never tasted better.

1/2 pound pasta of your choice
8 cups water
15-ounce can crushed tomatoes
5 ripe peaches, pitted and chopped
1/4 teaspoon cumin
1/4 teaspoon curry powder

Cook pasta in boiling water in a large pot for 8-10 minutes. Drain.
   Meanwhile, cook tomatoes, peaches, and spices in a small pot over
medium heat for 15 minutes. Serve warm sauce over the cooked pasta.

Total calories per serving: 278   Fat: 1 gram   Total Fat as % of Daily Value: 2%
Protein: 9 grams   Iron: 3 mg   Carbohydrates: 59 grams   Calcium: 43 mg
Dietary fiber: 4 grams   Sodium: 177 mg

PENNE WITH SUNDRIED TOMATOES, GARLIC, AND SPINACH

(Serves 4)

This quick-and-easy pasta dish is absolutely delicious!

1/2 pound penne or other pasta
8 cups water
1 cup sundried tomatoes (about 20-25), chopped
4 cloves garlic, minced
10-ounce box frozen chopped spinach, partially thawed
1/3 cup water
Salt and pepper to taste

Cook penne in boiling water in a large pot for 10 minutes and drain.

Meanwhile, in a large non-stick frying pan, sauté the remaining ingredients over medium heat for 10 minutes. Toss pasta with the tomato, garlic, and spinach mixture. Serve warm.

Total calories per serving: 269   Fat: 1 gram   Total Fat as % of Daily Value: 2%
Protein: 12 grams   Iron: 4 mg   Carbohydrates: 55 grams   Calcium: 134 mg
Dietary fiber: 3 grams   Sodium: 348 mg

SPINACH LASAGNA

(Serves 6)

Preparing this dish takes a little time but is well worth the effort.

1 pound lasagna noodles
5 quarts water
1 teaspoon oil
Medium onion, finely chopped
1/3 cup vegetable broth
1 pound soft tofu, crumbled
10-ounce package frozen chopped spinach, thawed
Two 15-ounce cans tomato sauce
1 teaspoon basil
1/2 teaspoon garlic powder
2 Tablespoons nutritional yeast (optional)

Cook noodles in boiling water for 10 minutes until tender. Drain.

In a separate large pan, sauté onion in oil over medium-high heat for 2 minutes. Add broth, tofu, and spinach. Sauté 6 minutes longer. Set aside.

In a small bowl, mix sauce with seasonings and yeast.

Preheat oven to 400 degrees. In a 13" x 9" x 2" baking pan put the following layers: 1/3 noodles, 1/3 tofu mixture, 1/3 tomato sauce then repeat the layers 2 more times. Bake 30 minutes at 400 degrees. Serve hot.

Total calories per serving: 406   Fat: 6 grams   Total Fat as % of Daily Value: 9%
Protein: 19 grams   Iron: 9 mg   Carbohydrates: 72 grams   Calcium: 185 mg
Dietary fiber: 5 grams   Sodium: 934 mg

UNIQUE LASAGNA

(Serves 6-8)

*This dish involves using several different pots and pans,
but is well worth the effort.*

10-ounce box lasagna noodles (about 12 noodles)
4 quarts water
2 pounds white potatoes, peeled and chopped
4 cups water
10-ounce box frozen chopped spinach
1/2 cup water
1 pound mushrooms (your choice of mushroom varieties),
   chopped
2 teaspoons oil
28-ounce jar of your favorite vegan pasta sauce

Cook noodles in 4 quarts boiling water in a large pot for 10 minutes until tender. Drain.

Meanwhile, cook potatoes in 4 cups boiling water in a medium-size pot for 15 minutes. Drain and mash potatoes.

Cook spinach in 1/2 cup water in a small pot over medium heat. Drain off any excess liquid.

Sauté mushrooms in oil in a large frying pan over medium heat for 5 minutes.

Preheat oven to 375 degrees. In a 13"x9"x2" pan place the following layers: 1/2 cooked noodles, 1/2 mashed potatoes, all of the cooked spinach, 1/2 pasta sauce, remaining cooked noodles, remaining mashed potatoes, all of the sautéed mushrooms, and remaining pasta sauce. Bake 30 minutes at 375 degrees and serve hot.

Total calories per serving: 460   Fat: 7 grams   Total Fat as % of Daily Value: 11%
Protein: 14 grams   Iron: 6 mg   Carbohydrates: 86 grams   Calcium: 132 mg
Dietary fiber: 9 grams   Sodium: 566 mg

THIN NOODLES WITH CITRUS SAUCE

(Serves 4)

Serve this delicious sauce over somen, udon, or cellophane noodles.

8 ounces thin noodles (somen, udon, cellophane, etc.)
8 cups water
16-ounce can grapefruit sections, drained
10.5-ounce can juice packed mandarin oranges (save juice)
2 Tablespoons cornstarch
1/3 cup water
1/4 teaspoon dried mint (optional)

Cook the noodles in 8 cups boiling water in a large pot for 8-10 minutes. Drain.

Meanwhile, pour drained grapefruit and mandarin oranges with their juice into a large non-stick frying pan. Dissolve cornstarch in 1/3 cup water and add to the citrus fruit. Add mint, if desired. Heat ingredients over medium heat for 3 minutes stirring constantly until sauce thickens. Serve warm over the cooked noodles.

Total calories per serving: 286   Fat: 1 gram   Total Fat as % of Daily Value: 2%
Protein: 8 grams   Iron: 1 mg   Carbohydrates: 63 grams   Calcium: 38 mg
Dietary fiber: 2 grams   Sodium: 106 mg

SPAGHETTI WITH MUSHROOM/TOMATO SAUCE
(Serves 6)

Serve this dish for lunch.

1 pound spaghetti, broken in half
5 quarts water
1/4 pound shiitake mushrooms, chopped
Small onion, finely chopped
1/2 teaspoon oregano
2 teaspoons oil
14-ounce can diced tomatoes in juice or whole tomatoes in
   juice, chopped

Cook pasta in boiling water in a large pot until done. Drain.

   Meanwhile, in a large non-stick frying pan sauté mushrooms, onion, and oregano in oil for 3 minutes over a medium-high heat. Add tomatoes and cooked spaghetti and cook 3 minutes longer. Serve warm.

Total calories per serving: 330   Fat: 3 grams   Total Fat as % of Daily Value: 5%
Protein: 11 grams   Iron: 4 mg   Carbohydrates: 65 grams   Calcium: 27 mg
Dietary fiber: 4 grams   Sodium: 270 mg

GRAVIES AND SAUCES

MUSHROOM GRAVY
(Makes about 2 cups -- 4 servings)

*Serve this gravy over your favorite burgers, loaf,
baked potatoes, or cooked grains.*

6-ounce package mushrooms (portabello or shiitake for
    example), finely chopped
Small onion, finely chopped
Pepper to taste
2 teaspoons oil
2 Tablespoons nutritional yeast
1/4 cup unbleached white flour
2 teaspoons tamari or soy sauce
1-1/2 cups water

Sauté the mushrooms, onion, and pepper in the oil in a large frying pan
over medium heat for 5 minutes. Add the remaining ingredients and
continue heating for 3 minutes, stirring until the gravy thickens. Serve
warm.

Total calories per 1/2 cup serving: 78   Fat: 3 grams   Total Fat as % of Daily Value: 5%
Protein: 3 grams   Iron: 1 mg   Carbohydrates: 11 grams   Calcium: 9 mg
Dietary fiber: 1 gram   Sodium: 170 mg

CHICKPEA GRAVY

(Makes about 4 cups -- 8 servings)

Serve this gravy over burgers, baked potatoes, and more.

Two 19-ounce cans chickpeas, rinsed and drained
1 cup water
1/4 cup fresh dill, finely chopped
2 Tablespoons tamari or soy sauce

Place half of the chickpeas in a food processor bowl. Add water and blend until creamy.

Pour the puréed chickpea mixture into a small pot. Add the remaining ingredients. Heat over medium heat for 5 minutes, stirring often.

Total calories per 1/2 cup serving: 148   Fat: 2 grams   Total Fat as % of Daily Value: 3%
Protein: 6 grams   Iron: 2 mg   Carbohydrates: 20 grams   Calcium: 42 mg
Dietary fiber: 7 grams   Sodium: 531 mg

MANGO/TOMATO/DATE SAUCE

(Makes about 3 cups -- Serves 6)

This sauce is visually beautiful when served.

2 ripe mangos — peeled, pitted, and chopped
14.5-ounce can whole tomatoes, chopped (keep liquid)
5 ounces pitted dates (about 16), chopped

Place all the ingredients in a medium-size pot. Cook for 10 minutes over medium-high heat. Serve sauce over cooked pasta, baked potatoes, or a cooked grain.

Total calories per 1/2 cup: 124   Fat: <1 gram   Total Fat as % of Daily Value: <1%
Protein: 1 gram   Iron: 1 mg   Carbohydrates: 32 grams   Calcium: 32 mg
Dietary fiber: 4 grams   Sodium: 114 mg

THICK TOMATO/KALE SAUCE

(Serves 3)

Serve this sauce over cooked pasta, baked potatoes, or a cooked grain.

14-ounce can diced tomatoes or whole tomatoes, chopped
1/2 pound fresh kale, rinsed and finely chopped
Small onion, finely chopped
2 Tablespoons lemon juice

Cook all the ingredients together in a large frying pan over medium heat for 10 minutes, stirring occasionally. Serve warm.

Total calories per serving: 90   Fat: 1 gram   Total Fat as % of Daily Value: 2%
Protein: 4 grams   Iron: 2 mg   Carbohydrates: 20 grams   Calcium: 80 mg
Dietary fiber: 6 grams   Sodium: 548 mg

TOMATO/SQUASH SAUCE

(Serves 5)

Enjoy this sweet tasting sauce.

28-ounce can whole tomatoes, quartered (keep liquid)
2 small yellow squash, finely chopped
Small onion, finely chopped
1 cup raisins
1/2 teaspoon cinnamon

Place all the ingredients in a medium-size pot and bring to a boil. Reduce heat to medium and cook 20 minutes. Serve sauce over cooked pasta or a baked potato.

Total calories per serving: 134   Fat: 1 gram   Total Fat as % of Daily Value: 2%
Protein: 3 grams   Iron: 2 mg   Carbohydrates: 33 grams   Calcium: 69 mg
Dietary fiber: 33 grams   Sodium: 265 mg

GRAINS

Main Dishes:

BARLEY BURGERS
(Makes 7 burgers)

These hearty burgers are absolutely delicious.

1 cup hulled barley
4 cups water
6-ounce can tomato paste
2 carrots, grated
1 stalk celery, finely chopped
1/2 teaspoon garlic powder
2 Tablespoons cornstarch

Bring the water to a boil in a medium-size pot. Add barley, reduce heat to medium, and cook covered 50 minutes until barley is tender. Drain any excess liquid.

Mix cooked barley with remaining ingredients in a large bowl. Form 7 burgers with your hands and cook in an oiled large frying pan over medium-high heat for 10 minutes on each side. Serve warm with lettuce on a whole grain bun.

Total calories per burger: 132   Fat: 1 gram   Total Fat as % of Daily Value: 2%
Protein: 4 grams   Iron: 2 mg   Carbohydrates: 28 grams   Calcium: 25 mg
Dietary fiber: 6 grams   Sodium: 207 mg

BARLEY AND BUTTERNUT SQUASH

(Serves 6)

Enjoy this sweet dish!

1-1/2 cups hulled barley
5 cups water
2 pounds butternut squash — peeled, seeds removed, and
    chopped into 1-inch cubes
1 cup raisins
2 cups apple juice
1/2 teaspoon clove powder

Bring the water to a boil in a covered medium-size pot. Add barley, reduce heat to medium and cook for 50 minutes. Drain any excess liquid.

Meanwhile, in a covered medium-size pot cook the squash, raisins, apple juice, and clove powder over medium heat for 35 minutes.

Combine cooked barley and squash mixtures together and serve warm.

Total calories per serving: 331   Fat: 2 grams   Total Fat as % of Daily Value: 3%
Protein: 9 grams   Iron: 3 mg   Carbohydrates: 76 grams   Calcium: 78 mg
Dietary fiber: 8 grams   Sodium: 19 mg

BASMATI RICE BURGERS

(Makes 12 burgers)

Serve 2 burgers per adult with vegan gravy or on whole grain buns with a slice of tomato and lettuce.

14-ounce box basmati rice (2-1/4 cups)
5 cups water
10-ounce box frozen peas
10-ounce box frozen corn kernels
1 teaspoon thyme
Salt and pepper to taste
4 Tablespoons cornstarch

Cook rice in boiling water in a medium-size covered pot for 15 minutes. Remove from the stove and allow to sit 10 minutes.

Meanwhile, cook the peas and corn per instructions on their packages and drain.

Mix cooked rice and vegetables together along with the remaining ingredients. Form 12 burgers and fry in a lightly oiled non-stick frying pan over medium-high heat for 3 minutes on each side. Serve warm.

Total calories per 2 burgers: 345   Fat: 1 gram   Total Fat as % of Daily Value: 2%
Protein: 9 grams   Iron: 4 mg   Carbohydrates: 65 grams   Calcium: 30 mg
Dietary fiber: 4 grams   Sodium: 47 mg

BULGUR STUFFED ACORN SQUASH

(Serves 4)

This delicious dish is a beautiful centerpiece on each plate.

2 medium acorn squash, sliced in half and seeds removed
2 cups water
1 cup bulgur
1 apple — cored, peeled, and chopped into 1-inch cubes
1/8 teaspoon cinnamon
2 cups apple juice

Preheat oven to 400 degrees. Place squash halves cut side up in a pan with water. Bake uncovered 1 hour or until squash is tender.

Meanwhile, in a separate medium-size covered pot heat bulgur, apples, and cinnamon in the juice over medium heat for 20 minutes. Stir occasionally to prevent sticking.

Spoon out cooked squash leaving a 1/4-inch thick shell. Mash the squash and mix it well with the cooked bulgur mixture. Re-stuff the acorn squash halves and serve 1 per person immediately. You can also reheat the squash halves and serve them at a later time.

Total calories per serving: 312   Fat: 1 gram   Total Fat as % of Daily Value: 2%
Protein: 7 grams   Iron: 3 mg   Carbohydrates: 76 grams   Calcium: 111 mg
Dietary fiber: 13 grams   Sodium: 24 mg

BULGUR/PEAS/TOMATO AND OLIVE STEW

(Serves 6)

Enjoy this hearty dish!

2 cups bulgur
10-ounce box frozen peas
Two 14-ounce cans whole tomatoes, chopped (keep juice)
4 cups water
3 ounces pitted black olives (about 15), drained and
    chopped
1 teaspoon dried basil

Place all the ingredients in a large non-stick pot. Bring to a boil, reduce heat, cover, and simmer for 30 minutes. Stir occasionally to prevent sticking. Serve warm.

Total calories per serving: 236   Fat: 3 grams   Total Fat as % of Daily Value: 5%
Protein: 10 grams   Iron: 3 mg   Carbohydrates: 48 grams   Calcium: 70 mg
Dietary fiber: 14 grams   Sodium: 312 mg

COUSCOUS LETTUCE ROLLS

(Serves 5 -- 4 each)

For variation, try pitted sweet cherries instead of the grapes.

10-ounce box couscous
2-1/4 cups water
1/2 pound seedless grapes, chopped in half
1/4 teaspoon cinnamon
Two one-pound heads romaine lettuce
Two 15-ounce cans tomato sauce

Bring water to a boil in a medium-size pot. Add couscous, cover, and turn off heat. Allow to sit 5 minutes. Add grapes and cinnamon to couscous. Stir well.

Preheat oven to 350 degrees. Remove 20 leaves from the heads of lettuce. Rinse leaves well. Place about 3 tablespoons of couscous mixture on each leaf and roll the leaves up, tucking ends under. Place stuffed leaves on a large baking pan. Cover stuffed leaves with sauce. Bake at 350 degrees for 20 minutes. Serve warm.

Total calories per serving: 322   Fat: 1 gram   Total Fat as % of Daily Value: 2%
Protein: 3 grams   Iron: 4 mg   Carbohydrates: 68 grams   Calcium: 109 mg
Dietary fiber: 15 grams   Sodium: 1049 mg

MILLET STEW
(Serves 6)

This stew is terrific on a cold evening.

2 cups millet (about 14 ounces)
5 cups water
3 stalks celery, chopped
3 carrots, peeled and chopped
1-1/2 pounds zucchini (2 medium), chopped
2 Tablespoons tamari or soy sauce
1/2 teaspoon garlic powder
Pepper to taste

Place all the ingredients in a large covered pot and cook for 30 minutes over medium-high heat or until done. Stir often and add more water if needed to prevent sticking. Serve warm.

Total calories per serving: 290   Fat: 3 grams   Total Fat as % of Daily Value: 5%
Protein: 10 grams   Iron: 3 mg   Carbohydrates: 57 grams   Calcium: 41 mg
Dietary fiber: 12 grams   Sodium: 372 mg

QUINOA AND EGGPLANT

(Serves 5)

This is a quick-and-easy grain-based meal.

12-ounce box quinoa (2 cups)
4 cups water
1 pound eggplant, peeled and chopped into 1-inch cubes
Small onion, finely chopped
1 teaspoon dried basil
Salt and pepper to taste
2 teaspoons oil
8 ounces tomato sauce

Cook quinoa in water in a medium-size covered pot over medium heat for 15 minutes. Meanwhile, sauté eggplant, onion, and seasonings in oil in a large non-stick frying pan over medium-high heat for 10 minutes. Add tomato sauce and cooked quinoa and sauté 5 minutes longer. Serve warm.

Total calories per serving: 315   Fat: 6 grams   Total Fat as % of Daily Value: 9%
Protein: 11 grams   Iron: 7 mg   Carbohydrates: 57 grams   Calcium: 57 mg
Dietary fiber: 4 grams   Sodium: 313 mg

QUINOA/SWEET POTATO PATTIES

(Makes 8 -- Serve 2 per person)

Enjoy these beautiful looking patties.

1-1/2 cups sweet potatoes, peeled and chopped
4 cups water
1 cup quinoa (half a 12-ounce box)
2 cups water
1/2 teaspoon cinnamon
2 teaspoons oil (for pan)

Place sweet potatoes in a medium-size pot with 4 cups water over high heat. Bring to a boil, reduce heat to medium, and cook 35 minutes or until the potatoes are done. Drain and mash potatoes.

Meanwhile, place the quinoa and 2 cups water in a separate medium-size pot. Bring to a boil, reduce heat to low, cover, and cook 15 minutes.

Mix mashed sweet potatoes and cooked quinoa together along with the cinnamon. Form 8 patties and place in a lightly oiled large frying pan over medium-high heat. Cook 5 minutes on each side and serve warm.

Total calories per serving: 128   Fat: 2 grams   Total Fat as % of Daily Value: 3%
Protein: 3 grams   Iron: 2 mg   Carbohydrates: 24 grams   Calcium: 23 mg
Dietary fiber: 2 grams   Sodium: 8 mg

Side Dishes:

SAUTÉED AMARANTH, PEAS, AND ONION
(Serves 6)

This side dish should be served like mashed potatoes.

1 cup amaranth
3 cups water
10-ounce box frozen peas
1 cup water
1 medium onion, finely chopped
1/2 teaspoon thyme
Salt and pepper to taste

Cook amaranth in 3 cups water in a medium-size covered pot for 25 minutes over medium heat.

Meanwhile, in a separate small pot, cook peas in 1 cup water for 4 minutes. Drain when done.

Mix the cooked amaranth together with the cooked peas and remaining ingredients. Pour into a lightly oiled frying pan over medium heat and brown, turning occasionally, for 12 minutes. Serve warm.

Total calories per serving: 185   Fat: 5 grams   Total Fat as % of Daily Value: 8%
Protein: 7 grams   Iron: 3 mg   Carbohydrates: 30 grams   Calcium: 64 mg
Dietary fiber: 2 grams   Sodium: 49 mg

BULGUR, CORN, AND GREENS

(Serves 4)

Enjoy this delicious blend of ingredients.

1 cup bulgur
2 cups water
10-ounce box frozen corn kernels
1/2 pound greens (kale or collards), rinsed and cut into
    bite-size pieces
1/2 teaspoon cumin
2 Tablespoons lemon juice

Cook bulgur in water in a large covered pot for 10 minutes over medium heat. Add remaining ingredients. Heat 10 minutes longer, stirring occasionally. Serve warm.

Total calories per serving: 193   Fat: 1 gram   Total Fat as % of Daily Value: 2%
Protein: 7 grams   Iron: 1 mg   Carbohydrates: 28 grams   Calcium: 19 mg
Dietary fiber: 10 grams   Sodium: 13 mg

GRAIN MEDLEY

(Serves 6)

Savor this grain and dried fruit mixture.

1-1/2 cups wild rice (about 8 ounces), rinsed
4 cups water
1 cup white basmati rice (about 6 ounces)
3 cups water
1 cup dried fruit (raisins, chopped apricots or prunes, for
    example)
1/2 teaspoon cinnamon

Cook wild rice in 4 cups water over medium-high heat in a large covered pot for 50 minutes or until tender. Drain any excess liquid.

In a separate covered medium-size pot, cook the basmati rice, dried fruit, and cinnamon in 3 cups water over medium-high heat for 15 minutes. Remove from the stove and allow the mixture to sit covered for 10 minutes longer. Combine the two grains together, mix well, and serve warm as a side dish.

Total calories per serving: 312   Fat: 1 gram   Total Fat as % of Daily Value: 2%
Protein: 9 grams   Iron: 3 mg   Carbohydrates: 69 grams   Calcium: 28 mg
Dietary fiber: 2 grams   Sodium: 6 mg

ISRAELI COUSCOUS/ FARFEL DISH
(Serves 8)

The toasted couscous and farfel used in this dish can be found in kosher supermarkets and gourmet markets.

1 large onion, chopped
2 teaspoons oil
7 cups vegetable broth
Salt and pepper to taste
8.8-ounce package toasted couscous
8.8-ounce package toasted farfel

Sauté onion in oil in a large pot over medium heat for 2 minutes. Add remaining ingredients and simmer 10 minutes. Stir often to prevent sticking. Serve warm.

Total calories per serving: 291   Fat: 4 grams   Total Fat as % of Daily Value: 6%
Protein: 9 grams   Iron: <1 mg   Carbohydrates: 57 grams   Calcium: 11 mg
Dietary fiber: 5 grams   Sodium: 392 mg

SAUTÉED MILLET AND BROCCOLI WITH RAISINS
(Serves 5)

This side dish should be served the same way you would serve mashed potatoes.

1 cup millet
3 cups water
1 pound broccoli, chopped into bite-size pieces
1/2 cup raisins
3/4 cup vegetable broth

Cook millet in water in a covered medium-size pot over medium-low heat for 30 minutes. Stir occasionally and add water if needed to prevent sticking.

In a large frying pan, sauté broccoli and raisins in the vegetable broth for 5 minutes. Add the cooked millet and stir 2 minutes longer. Serve warm.

Total calories per serving: 223   Fat: 2 grams   Total Fat as % of Daily Value: 3%
Protein: 8 grams   Iron: 2 mg   Carbohydrates: 45 grams   Calcium: 54 mg
Dietary fiber: 9 grams   Sodium: 61 mg

VEGGIE AND RICE PILAF

(Serves 6)

Enjoy this simple, beautiful looking, pilaf.

14 ounces white basmati rice (about 2-1/4 cups)
5 cups water
6 ounces dried apricots, chopped (about 1 cup)
10-ounce box frozen peas
1/4 cup shredded coconut
1/2 cup vegetable broth

Cook rice in water in a medium-size covered pot over medium heat for about 15 minutes or until done. Remove from stove and allow to sit covered for 5 minutes.

Sauté cooked rice and remaining ingredients in a large non-stick pot over medium-heat for 5 minutes. Serve warm.

Total calories per serving: 369   Fat: 2 grams   Total Fat as % of Daily Value: 3%
Protein: 9 grams   Iron: 5 mg   Carbohydrates: 80 grams   Calcium: 44 mg
Dietary fiber: 5 grams   Sodium: 135 mg

BEANS

Main Dishes:

BEAN BALLS
(Serves 6-8)

This delicious alternative to meatballs can be served with tomato sauce over pasta or with tomato sauce on Italian bread as a sandwich.

Two 15-ounce cans kidney beans (about 3-1/3 cups
    cooked) — rinsed, drained, and mashed
2 stalks celery, finely chopped
2 carrots, peeled and grated
1/2 small onion, finely chopped
1 teaspoon oregano
2/3 cup unbleached white flour

Stir all the ingredients together in a large bowl. Form 16 three-inch round balls. Fry bean balls in lightly oiled large frying pan over medium-high heat until brown on all sides (about 15 minutes). Serve warm.

Total calories per serving: 193   Fat: 2 grams   Total Fat as % of Daily Value: 3%
Protein: 9 grams   Iron: 2 mg   Carbohydrates: 35 grams   Calcium: 53 mg
Dietary fiber: 9 grams   Sodium: 509 mg

QUICK BLACK BEAN BURRITOS

(Serves 5 -- two per person)

Tortillas are popular flat Mexican bread.
Look for tortillas that do not contain whey. Roll the tortillas around
the bean filling to make delicious burritos.

Two 15-ounce cans black beans (about 3-1/3 cups pre-cooked), rinsed and drained
16-ounce package frozen mixed vegetables
Small onion, finely chopped
Package of ten wheat tortillas
16-ounce jar salsa

Sauté black beans and vegetables in a large pot over medium heat for 15 minutes. Meanwhile, heat tortillas on a baking pan in a 300 degree oven for 5 minutes.

Put 1/10th of the black bean/vegetable mixture on each tortilla with a heaping tablespoon of salsa. Roll up the tortillas before serving.

Total calories per serving: 456   Fat: 6 grams   Total Fat as % of Daily Value: 11%
Protein: 19 grams   Iron: 5 mg   Carbohydrates: 80 grams   Calcium: 135 mg
Dietary fiber: 8 grams   Sodium: 1077 mg

CHICKPEAS, POTATOES, AND ONION

(Serves 5)

Savor this dish on a chilly evening.

1-1/2 pounds white potatoes, peeled and thinly sliced
1 large onion, finely chopped
2 Tablespoons oil
19-ounce can chickpeas, rinsed and drained
1/2 teaspoon turmeric
Salt and pepper to taste

Cook potatoes and onion in oil in a large covered non-stick frying pan over medium-high heat for 20 minutes. Stir occasionally.

Add chickpeas and seasoning and continue cooking covered for 10 minutes longer, stirring occasionally. Serve warm.

Total calories per serving: 261   Fat: 8 grams   Total Fat as % of Daily Value: 12%
Protein: 7 grams   Iron: 3 mg   Carbohydrates: 43 grams   Calcium: 46 mg
Dietary fiber: 8 grams   Sodium: 143 mg

SPICY MANDARIN CHICKPEAS

(Serves 4)

Serve this delicious combination of ingredients over a bed of rice.

Two 19-ounce cans chickpeas, rinsed and drained
Two 10.5-ounce cans mandarin oranges, drained
1/4 cup strawberry jam
2 Tablespoons spicy brown mustard
1/2 teaspoon cayenne

Heat all the ingredients in a medium-size pot over medium heat for 10 minutes. Serve warm.

Total calories per serving: 357   Fat: 6 grams   Total Fat as % of Daily Value: 9%
Protein: 11 grams   Iron: 4 mg   Carbohydrates: 69 grams   Calcium: 110 mg
Dietary fiber: 15 grams   Sodium: 670 mg

CHILI
(Serves 6)

Enjoy this unique chili served over a bed of rice or with tortillas.

2 pounds yams or sweet potatoes, peeled and chopped
Two 14-1/2-ounce cans whole tomatoes (keep liquid)
1 cup water
Three 15-ounce cans kidney beans (about 5 cups cooked),
    rinsed and drained
2 jalapeño peppers, seeds carefully removed and discarded,
    and finely chopped
2 Tablespoons chili powder
1 teaspoon cumin
Salt and pepper to taste

Simmer yams or sweet potatoes with whole tomatoes and water in a
covered large pot over medium-low heat for 30 minutes. Add remaining
ingredients and cook uncovered over medium heat for 30 minutes longer.
Serve warm.

Total calories per serving: 366   Fat: 2 grams   Total Fat as % of Daily Value: 3%
Protein: 15 grams   Iron: 5 mg   Carbohydrates: 77 grams   Calcium: 144 mg
Dietary fiber: 18 grams   Sodium: 1002 mg

KIDNEY BEAN AND PEACH CAKES
(Makes 5 burgers)

Here's a unique burger you're sure to enjoy!

15-ounce can kidney beans, rinsed and drained
1-pound can peach halves, drained
1 cup unbleached white flour
1/4 teaspoon cumin
Salt and pepper to taste
2 teaspoons oil (for pan)

Place all the ingredients except the oil in a food processor bowl. Blend for 2 minutes. Pour batter to form 5 burgers in an oiled large frying pan. Fry over medium-high heat for 5 minutes on each side. Serve warm on whole grain bread with lettuce and a slice of tomato.

Total calories per burger: 216   Fat: 2 grams   Total Fat as % of Daily Value: 3%
Protein: 8 grams   Iron: 2 mg   Carbohydrates: 42 grams   Calcium: 32 mg
Dietary fiber: 6 grams   Sodium: 300 mg

LENTIL/SPINACH/POTATO STEW
(Serves 4)

Enjoy this hearty stew!

3 cups cooked greenish-brown or red lentils
4 medium-size white potatoes, chopped into small cubes
    and cooked
1/2 cup water
10-ounce box frozen chopped spinach
Small onion, finely chopped
3 Tablespoons lemon juice
Salt and pepper to taste

Place all the ingredients in a large frying pan and cook over medium heat for 15 minutes, stirring often. Serve warm.

Total calories per serving: 349   Fat: 1 gram   Total Fat as % of Daily Value: 2%
Protein: 19 grams   Iron: 8 mg   Carbohydrates: 70 grams   Calcium: 151 mg
Dietary fiber: 12 grams   Sodium: 75 mg

BEAN TACOS

(Serves 6 -- two per person)

When in a rush, try these simple homemade tacos.

12 taco or tostada shells
Two 16-ounce cans fat-free vegan refried beans
Small head of lettuce, shredded
2 ripe tomatoes, chopped
16-ounce jar salsa

Heat taco or tostada shells for 5 minutes in a 350 degree oven.

Meanwhile, warm up refried beans in a medium-size pot over medium heat for 3 minutes.

Fill taco shells or top tostada shells with heated beans, lettuce, and tomatoes. Top with salsa before serving.

Total calories per serving: 310   Fat: 8 grams   Total Fat as % of Daily Value: 12%
Protein: 13 grams   Iron: 4 mg   Carbohydrates: 51 grams   Calcium: 142 mg
Dietary fiber: 9 grams   Sodium: 1423 mg

YELLOW SPLIT PEA STEW

(Serves 5)

Serve this delicious hearty stew over a cooked grain.

1-1/2 cups yellow split peas
4 cups water
3 green bell peppers, chopped and seeds removed
1 large onion, chopped
2/3 cup shredded coconut
1 cup water

Place split peas and 4 cups water in a medium-size pot and bring to a boil. Reduce heat, then cook 25 minutes. Drain any excess liquid.

Sauté peppers, onion, and coconut with water in a large non-stick frying pan over medium heat for 10 minutes. Add the cooked split peas and sauté 5 minutes longer. Serve warm.

Total calories per serving: 261   Fat: 4 grams   Total Fat as % of Daily Value: 6%
Protein: 16 grams   Iron: 3 mg   Carbohydrates: 42 grams   Calcium: 43 mg
Dietary fiber: 5 grams   Sodium: 13 mg

Side Dishes:

MIXED BEANS AND GREENS
(Serves 5)

You are encouraged to experiment with different varieties of beans and green leafy vegetables in this recipe.

Two 15-ounce cans beans (black-eyed peas, navy, kidney, chickpeas, for example), drained and rinsed
2 pounds shredded greens (kale, bok choy, collards, for example)
1/4 cup fresh lemon juice
1/2 cup water
1/4 teaspoon dried dill weed

Sauté all the ingredients in a large pot over medium-high heat for 10 minutes. Serve warm as a side dish or over a cooked grain such as rice or bulgur.

Total calories per serving (black-eyed peas and kale): 184   Fat: 2 grams
Total Fat as % of Daily Value: 3%   Protein: 13 grams   Iron: 3 mg
Carbohydrates: 31 grams   Calcium: 114 mg   Dietary fiber: 16 grams   Sodium: 32 mg

BEANS AND RICE MEDLEY

(Serves 4)

Choosing different color bell peppers adds a nice touch to this dish.

Half 14-ounce box white basmati rice (about 1 cup)
1-3/4 cups water
15-ounce can black beans (about 1-2/3 cups cooked),
    rinsed and drained
10-ounce box frozen corn kernels
2 large bell peppers (any color), finely chopped and seeds
    removed
1/2 teaspoon cumin

Cook rice in boiling water for 15 minutes in a covered medium-size pot. Turn heat off and allow rice to sit covered for another 5 minutes.

Meanwhile, in a separate medium-size pot, heat the remaining ingredients over medium heat for 15 minutes. Stir once in a while. Combine cooked rice with bean mixture and serve warm.

Total calories per serving: 403   Fat: 2 grams   Total Fat as % of Daily Value: 3%
Protein: 16 grams   Iron: 5 mg   Carbohydrates: 69 grams   Calcium: 47 mg
Dietary fiber: 7 grams   Sodium: 200 mg

BLACK BEAN/ WATERCRESS SAUTÉ

(Serves 4)

Adding both lemon juice and lemon zest to this dish adds to the flavor.

1/2 pound watercress (about 2 large bunches), thick stems removed
1/2 lemon, seeds removed and minced (including rind)
1/3 cup vegetable broth
1/2 small onion, minced
15-ounce can black beans (about 1-2/3 cups cooked), rinsed and drained

Sauté all the ingredients in a large frying pan over medium heat for 8 minutes. Serve warm.

Total calories per serving: 155   Fat: 1 gram   Total Fat as % of Daily Value: 2%
Protein: 11 grams   Iron: 2 mg   Carbohydrates: 29 grams   Calcium: 106 mg
Dietary fiber: 5 grams   Sodium: 262 mg

CHICKPEA DELIGHT

(Serves 4)

Serve this as a cold side dish.

15-ounce can chickpeas (about 1-2/3 cups cooked), rinsed and drained
6 ounces plain or lemon soy yogurt (about 3/4 cup)
2 medium ripe tomatoes, finely chopped
1 teaspoon cumin

Mix all the ingredients together in a medium-size bowl and refrigerate at least 30 minutes before serving.

Total calories per serving: 148   Fat: 4 grams   Total Fat as % of Daily Value: 6%
Protein: 7 grams   Iron: 2 mg   Carbohydrates: 23 grams   Calcium: 46 mg
Dietary fiber: 7 grams   Sodium: 285 mg

SWEET FAVA BEANS
(Serves 4)

Here's a quick and easy side dish.

19-ounce can fava beans, rinsed and drained
8-ounce can no salt added tomato sauce
1/4 cup molasses
1/4 teaspoon cinnamon

Heat all the ingredients together in a medium-size pot over medium-high heat for 10 minutes. Serve warm.

Total calories per serving: 181   Fat: <1 gram   Total Fat as % of Daily Value: <1%
Protein: 7 grams   Iron: 3 mg   Carbohydrates: 37 grams   Calcium: 88 mg
Dietary fiber: 6 grams   Sodium: 174 mg

FAVA BEANS AND CORN
(Serves 4)

This is a beautiful, yet simple side dish.

19-ounce can fava beans, rinsed and drained
10-ounce box frozen corn kernels
3 Tablespoons lemon juice
3 Tablespoons water

Heat all the ingredients together in a medium-size pot over medium-high heat for 10 minutes. Serve warm.

Total calories per serving: 182   Fat: 1 gram   Total Fat as % of Daily Value: 2%
Protein: 9 grams   Iron: 1 mg   Carbohydrates: 22 grams   Calcium: 21 mg
Dietary fiber: 7 grams   Sodium: 156 mg

MEAT ALTERNATIVES

Seitan or Gluten Main Dishes:

'CHICKEN' AND VEGETABLES
(Serves 8)

Enjoy this hearty, stew-like dish.

2 pounds white potatoes, peeled and chopped into bite-size
    pieces
Small onion, finely chopped
1-1/2 cups vegetable broth
1 pound chicken-style wheat meat (gluten), chopped into
    bite-size pieces
10-ounce box frozen peas

Heat potatoes, onion, and broth in a large covered pot over medium-high
heat for 20 minutes. Add wheat meat and peas and continue cooking
another 10 minutes. Serve warm.

Total calories per serving: 174   Fat: 1 gram   Total Fat as % of Daily Value: 2%
Protein: 12 grams   Iron: 2 mg   Carbohydrates: 32 grams   Calcium: 41 mg
Dietary fiber: 7 grams   Sodium: 297 mg

GLAZED 'CHICKEN'

(Serves 4)

You will relish this mock chicken dish.

1 pound chicken-style wheat meat (gluten), chopped into
    bite-size pieces
10.5-ounce can mandarin oranges, drained
10-ounce jar apricot jam
1/4 cup molasses
2 Tablespoons orange juice
1/4 teaspoon cayenne pepper

Preheat oven to 400 degrees. Meanwhile, spread out chopped 'chicken'
in a 9"x9"x2" square pan. Spread oranges on top. Next, mix remaining
ingredients together and pour mixture over the 'chicken' and oranges.

Bake 'chicken' in an oven at 400 degrees for 20 minutes. Serve warm
over a bed of rice.

Total calories per serving (without rice): 372   Fat: <1 gram   Total Fat as % of Daily
Value: <1%   Protein: 16 grams   Iron: 4 mg   Carbohydrates: 79 grams
Calcium: 128 mg   Dietary fiber: 8 grams   Sodium: 371 mg

SEITAN CHILI
(Serves 4)

Here's a quick and easy version of hearty vegetarian chili.

8-ounce package seitan, drained and cubed
Small onion, finely chopped
2 teaspoons oil
Two 15-ounce cans kidney beans, drained
14.5-ounce can whole tomatoes, chopped
1-1/2 teaspoons chili powder
1/2 teaspoon cumin
1/2 teaspoon oregano

Sauté seitan and onion in oil in a large frying pan over medium-high heat for 5 minutes. Add remaining ingredients and continue cooking 12 more minutes. Serve warm over baked potatoes or rice.

Total calories per serving (without rice): 258   Fat: 4 grams   Total Fat as % of Daily Value: 6%   Protein: 20 grams   Iron: 4 mg   Carbohydrates: 38 grams   Calcium: 40 mg Dietary fiber: 12 grams   Sodium: 1215 mg

SAUTÉED SEITAN AND CORN
(Serves 3)

Serve this dish over mashed potatoes or rice.

8-ounce package seitan, drained and cubed
10-ounce package frozen corn kernels
Small jalapeño pepper, minced
1/3 cup vegetable broth

Sauté all the ingredients in a medium-size pot for 5 minutes over medium-high heat. Serve warm.

Total calories per serving: 146   Fat: 2 grams   Total Fat as % of Daily Value: 3%
Protein: 14 grams   Iron: 1 mg   Carbohydrates: 3 grams   Calcium: 2 mg
Dietary fiber: 3 grams   Sodium: 455 mg

SEITAN STEW

(Serves 6)

This hearty dish is absolutely delicious!

2 pounds potatoes, peeled and chopped into 1-inch cubes
1 pound carrots, peeled and finely chopped
4 cups water
Two 8-ounce packages seitan, drained and chopped into
    1-inch cubes
2 stalks celery, chopped
Small onion, finely chopped
2 teaspoons oil
Two 15-ounce cans vegan creamed corn
1-1/2 teaspoons marjoram

Cook potatoes and carrots in boiling water in large pot for 15 minutes.
Drain.

Meanwhile, sauté seitan, celery, and onion in oil in a large frying pan
over medium-high heat for 5 minutes. Add cooked potatoes and carrots.
Add creamed corn and marjoram. Continue cooking 10 minutes longer.
Serve warm.

Total calories per serving: 321   Fat: 3 grams   Total Fat as % of Daily Value: 5%
Protein: 17 grams   Iron: 3 mg   Carbohydrates: 62 grams   Calcium: 43 mg
Dietary fiber: 6 grams   Sodium: 852 mg

KOREAN BARBECUED SEITAN
(Serves 4)

Thanks to Reed Mangels, Ph.D., R.D., for sharing this delicious recipe!

Two 8-ounce packages seitan, drained and cut into 1/2-inch thick strips
1 Tablespoon toasted sesame seeds
1 Tablespoon sesame oil
1 Tablespoon maple syrup or apple juice
1 teaspoon minced garlic
1/4 teaspoon ginger powder
1 medium onion, chopped
3 cups warm cooked brown rice
20-32 lettuce leaves
Salsa or Korean hot pepper paste (available in some Oriental markets), to taste

Combine sesame seeds, oil, sweetener, spices, and onion in a glass baking dish. Add the seitan strips and toss to coat with the marinade. Cover and refrigerate 2-6 hours, stirring occasionally.

Heat a non-stick frying pan over medium-high heat and add the seitan mixture and marinade. Cook, stirring constantly, about 5 minutes.

To serve, place about 3/4 cup cooked rice, 5-8 lettuce leaves, and a fourth of the seitan on each plate. To eat, fill a lettuce leaf with rice, seitan, and salsa or hot pepper paste to taste. Roll up and eat with your fingers.

Total calories per serving (with 1 TB salsa): 310   Fat: 7 grams
Total Fat as % of Daily Value: 11%   Protein: 20 grams   Iron: 3 mg
Carbohydrates: 41 grams   Calcium: 73 mg   Dietary fiber: 4 grams   Sodium: 720 mg

Tempeh Main Dishes:

SAUTÉED CABBAGE AND TEMPEH WITH RAISINS AND PEANUTS
(Serves 4)

Enjoy this hearty meal.

8-ounce package tempeh, finely cubed
2 teaspoons oil
Small head green cabbage (about 2-1/2 pounds), shredded
1/2 cup raisins
2 Tablespoons shelled roasted peanuts
Salt and pepper to taste

Sauté tempeh in oil in large non-stick frying pan over medium-high heat for 5 minutes. Add remaining ingredients and continue to sauté for 10 minutes. Serve over a bed of rice.

Total calories per serving: 281   Fat: 9 grams   Total Fat as % of Daily Value: 14%
Protein: 16 grams   Iron: 3 mg   Carbohydrates: 40 grams   Calcium: 199 mg
Dietary fiber: 6 grams   Sodium: 57 mg

CURRIED TEMPEH
AND CARROTS

(Serves 3)

This quick-and-easy main dish is absolutely delicious!
Serve over a cooked grain of your choice.

8-ounce package tempeh, chopped into 1-inch cubes
1 pound carrots, peeled and finely chopped
2 teaspoons curry powder
Salt to taste
2 teaspoons oil

Sauté ingredients in a large non-stick frying pan for 10 minutes over medium heat. Serve warm.

Total calories per serving: 242   Fat: 9 grams   Total Fat as % of Daily Value: 14%
Protein: 16 grams   Iron: 2 mg   Carbohydrates: 28 grams   Calcium: 110 mg
Dietary fiber: 4 grams   Sodium: 57 mg

ITALIAN ORZO AND TEMPEH SAUCE
(Serves 5)

This tempeh sauce can also be served over rice.

16-ounce package orzo (rice-shaped pasta)
4 quarts water
8-ounce package tempeh, cubed
2 teaspoons oil
10-ounce package frozen peas or 2 cups fresh peas
15-ounce can tomato sauce

Cook orzo in boiling water in a large pot for 10 minutes. Drain.

Sauté tempeh in oil in a medium-size pot over medium heat for 5 minutes. Add peas and tomato sauce. Reduce heat and simmer 5 more minutes. Serve sauce over orzo.

Total calories per serving: 428   Fat: 9 grams   Total Fat as % of Daily Value: 14%
Protein: 21 grams   Iron: 3 mg   Carbohydrates: 71 grams   Calcium: 116 mg
Dietary fiber: 7 grams   Sodium: 574 mg

QUICK SLOPPY JOES
(Serves 5)

Serve this dish on whole wheat buns or over baked potatoes.

Small onion, chopped
2 teaspoons oil
Two 8-ounce packages tempeh, grated
2 teaspoons chili powder
1/2 teaspoon garlic powder
1/4 teaspoon salt
6-ounce can tomato paste
2 cups water

Sauté onion in oil in a large frying pan over medium heat for 2 minutes. Add tempeh and stir-fry 5 minutes longer.

Reduce heat, add remaining ingredients, and simmer 5 minutes. Serve warm.

Total calories per serving: 234   Fat: 9 grams   Total Fat as % of Daily Value: 14%
Protein: 19 grams   Iron: 3 mg   Carbohydrates: 24 grams   Calcium: 103 mg
Dietary fiber: 2 grams   Sodium: 400 mg

SAUTÉED TEMPEH WITH APPLES AND ONIONS

(Serves 3)

Serve this dish over a bed of rice.

2 teaspoons oil
8-ounce package tempeh, cubed
2 medium onions, sliced in rings
2 apples — peeled, cored, and chopped
Salt to taste

Heat oil in a large non-stick frying pan over medium-high heat. Add remaining ingredients and sauté for 10 minutes. Serve warm.

Total calories per serving: 251   Fat: 9 grams   Total Fat as % of Daily Value: 14%
Protein: 15 grams   Iron: 2 mg   Carbohydrates: 31 grams   Calcium: 87 mg
Dietary fiber: 2 grams   Sodium: 7 mg

TEMPEH WITH LEMONY CHINESE CABBAGE

(Serves 3)

Enjoy the rich, fresh lemony taste of this dish.

8-ounce package tempeh, chopped into 1-inch cubes
2 teaspoons oil
1 lemon, juiced (save rind)
1 Tablespoon lemon rind, minced
5 cups shredded Chinese cabbage
Salt and pepper to taste

Sauté tempeh in oil for 5 minutes in a large non-stick frying pan over medium-high heat. Add remaining ingredients and sauté 10 more minutes. Serve over cooked rice.

Total calories per serving: 204   Fat: 9 grams   Total Fat as % of Daily Value: 14%
Protein: 17 grams   Iron: 3 mg   Carbohydrates: 16 grams   Calcium: 189 mg
Dietary fiber: 1 grams   Sodium: 32 mg

TEMPEH MUSHROOM CASSEROLE

(Serves 4)

This dish is absolutely delicious.

1 cup hulled barley or brown rice
2-1/2 cups water
8-ounce package tempeh, cubed
Medium onion, finely chopped
1/2 cup chopped mushrooms (any variety)
1/2 cup chopped celery
1/2 teaspoon garlic powder
1/2 teaspoon cumin
1/2 teaspoon curry powder
1 Tablespoon oil
1-1/2 cups water
1/4 cup nutritional yeast
2 Tablespoons tamari or soy sauce
3 Tablespoons unbleached white flour

Cook barley or brown rice in water about 1 hour until done.

Meanwhile, sauté tempeh, onion, mushrooms, celery, and seasonings in oil in a large non-stick pot over medium heat for 10 minutes.

Preheat oven to 350 degrees. Add cooked barley or rice to tempeh mixture and pour into a 2-quart round baking dish.

Mix water, yeast, tamari or soy sauce, and flour together in a jar by shaking well. Pour over tempeh/rice mixture. Bake 30 minutes at 350 degrees. Serve warm.

Total calories per serving: 360   Fat: 9 grams   Total Fat as % of Daily Value: 14%
Protein: 21 grams   Iron: 4 mg   Carbohydrates: 54 grams   Calcium: 86 mg
Dietary fiber: 8 grams   Sodium: 526 mg

TEMPEH/PEAR CURRY

(Serves 3)

Creatively blending tempeh with fruit and curry powder
creates a delicious meal.

8-ounce package tempeh, chopped into 1-inch cubes
2 teaspoons oil
2 pears — cored, peeled, and finely chopped
1/2 cup raisins or other chopped dried fruit
1/4 cup orange juice
1/2 teaspoon curry powder

Sauté tempeh in oil in a large non-stick frying pan over medium-high heat
for 5 minutes. Add remaining ingredients and stir-fry 5 more minutes.
Serve over a bed of rice.

Total calories per serving: 353   Fat: 10 grams   Total Fat as % of Daily Value: 17%
Protein: 16 grams   Iron: 3 mg   Carbohydrates: 58 grams   Calcium: 103 mg
Dietary fiber: 6 grams   Sodium: 8 mg

TEMPEH, POTATOES, AND PEAS

(Serves 5)

Enjoy this hearty dish.

2 pounds white potatoes, peeled and chopped into 1-inch
    cubes
10-ounce box frozen peas
6 cups water
8-ounce package tempeh, chopped into 1-inch cubes
2 teaspoons oil
1 teaspoon dried dill weed
1 Tablespoon nutritional yeast
Salt and pepper to taste (optional)
2 Tablespoons lemon juice

Bring water to a boil in a large pot. Add potatoes, reduce heat to
medium-high and cook 15 minutes. Next, add peas and cook 5 minutes
longer. Drain.

Sauté tempeh in oil in a large non-stick frying pan over medium-high
heat for 5 minutes. Add cooked potatoes and peas along with remaining
ingredients. Sauté 3 minutes longer. Serve over a bed of rice.

Total calories per serving: 298   Fat: 6 grams   Total Fat as % of Daily Value: 9%
Protein: 16 grams   Iron: 3 mg   Carbohydrates: 49 grams   Calcium: 69 mg
Dietary fiber: 5 grams   Sodium: 64 mg

TEMPEH STUFFED POTATOES

(Serves 5)

Although it takes a while to prepare this dish, the end result is well worth the effort.

5 baking potatoes (about 3 pounds), scrubbed
8-ounce package tempeh, chopped into 1-inch cubes
Small onion, finely chopped
1/8 teaspoon garlic powder
1/8 teaspoon cumin
2 teaspoons oil
1/2 cup boiling water

Preheat oven to 400 degrees. Bake potatoes about 1 hour or until done. Remove from oven.

Meanwhile, in a separate large non-stick frying pan, sauté tempeh, onion, and seasonings in oil over medium-high heat for 10 minutes.

When the potatoes are done, split them in half lengthwise. Scoop out the cooked potato leaving a 1/4-inch shell. Mash the potatoes with the water and mix in the tempeh mixture. Stuff the mixture into the potato shells and serve 2 halves per person immediately. You can also reheat the stuffed potatoes and serve at another time.

Total calories per serving: 332   Fat: 6 grams   Total Fat as % of Daily Value: 9%
Protein: 13 grams   Iron: 4 mg   Carbohydrates: 60 grams   Calcium: 65 mg
Dietary fiber: 5 grams   Sodium: 19 mg

Tofu Main Dishes:

BULGUR/TOFU LOAF
(Serves 8)

This loaf is delicious served with steamed broccoli.

Medium onion, finely chopped
2 stalks celery, chopped
1/2 cup fresh parsley, minced
1/2 teaspoon Italian seasoning
1/4 teaspoon garlic, minced
2 teaspoons oil
15-ounce can tomato sauce
1 cup bulgur
2 cups water
2 Tablespoons cornstarch
1 pound firm tofu, crumbled

Sauté onion, celery, parsley, Italian seasoning, and garlic in oil in a large pot over medium heat for 2 minutes. Add sauce, bulgur, and water. Cook over medium-low heat for 25 minutes until bulgur is cooked.

Preheat oven to 350 degrees. Add cornstarch and crumbled tofu to mixture. Mix well. Press into a 9-1/4"x5-1/4"x3" non-stick loaf pan. Bake 30 minutes at 350 degrees. Allow to cool before slicing.

Total calories per serving: 183   Fat: 6 grams   Total Fat as % of Daily Value: 9%
Protein: 12 grams   Iron: 7 mg   Carbohydrates: 23 grams   Calcium: 142 mg
Dietary fiber: 6 grams   Sodium: 344 mg

CAJUN-SPICED TOFU BURGERS

(Makes 6)

These burgers are a bit spicy. If you prefer a milder flavor, simply reduce by half the amount of Cajun seasoning used.

19 ounces silken firm tofu (about 1-1/4 pounds), drained
2 carrots, peeled and grated
2 stalks celery, finely chopped
8-ounce can water chestnuts, drained
1-1/2 cups fine bread crumbs or matzo meal
2 teaspoons Cajun seasoning
1 teaspoon salt (optional)
2 teaspoons oil (for pan)

Place ingredients (except oil) in a food processor cup and blend until well mixed.

Heat oil over medium-high heat in a large non-stick frying pan. Form 6 large burgers with mixture and brown burgers for 10 minutes on each side. Serve warm with lettuce on whole wheat buns. Cold leftovers are also delicious.

Total calories per burger: 206   Fat: 5 grams   Total Fat as % of Daily Value: 8%
Protein: 10 grams   Iron: 3 mg   Carbohydrates: 30 grams   Calcium: 100 mg
Dietary fiber: 1 grams   Sodium: 286 mg

TOFU AND CRUCIFEROUS VEGETABLES

(Serves 6)

This colorful dish can be served alone or over a cooked grain.

1/2 small head cauliflower (about 1 pound), cored and
   chopped into bite-size pieces
1 pound broccoli, chopped into bite-size pieces
8 Brussels sprouts, ends cut off and chopped into bite-size
   pieces
1/2 small head red cabbage (about 3/4 pound), cored and
   chopped
1 cup vegetable broth
1 pound tofu, drained and cut into 1-inch cubes

Place all the ingredients (except the tofu) in a large pot. Cook over
medium-high heat for 8 minutes, stirring occasionally. Add the tofu and
cook 5 minutes longer, stirring occasionally. Serve warm.

Total calories per serving: 133   Fat: 4 grams   Total Fat as % of Daily Value: 6%
Protein: 12 grams   Iron: 6 mg   Carbohydrates: 17 grams   Calcium: 175 mg
Dietary fiber: 5 grams   Sodium: 100 mg

BAKED TOFU AND SPINACH

(Serves 6)

Try this unique dish.

Two 10-ounce boxes frozen chopped spinach
Two 10.5-ounce packages lite tofu, crumbled
Small onion, minced
2 Tablespoons vegan 'bacon' bits
3 Tablespoons nutritional yeast
1 Tablespoon tamari or soy sauce

Preheat oven to 450 degrees. Cook spinach according to the directions on the box. Drain well.

Place cooked spinach in a food processor cup and add the remaining ingredients. Blend well.

Pour mixture into a non-stick 9-inch pie pan. Bake at 450 degrees for 50 minutes. Allow to cool for 10 minutes, slice, and serve.

Total calories per serving: 75   Fat: 1 gram   Total Fat as % of Daily Value: 2%
Protein: 10 grams   Iron: 2 mg   Carbohydrates: 8 grams   Calcium: 162 mg
Dietary fiber: 2 grams   Sodium: 319 mg

SEASONED TOFU OVER SOMEN NOODLES

(Serves 3)

An Asian-style dish with delicious flavor.

1 pound tofu, drained and chopped into 1-inch cubes
2 teaspoons oil
1/4 teaspoon coriander
1/4 teaspoon cumin
1/4 teaspoon ginger powder
1 teaspoon tamari or soy sauce
8-ounce package somen noodles
2 quarts water

Sauté tofu with seasonings in oil in a large non-stick frying pan over medium-high heat for 8 minutes.

Meanwhile, bring the water to a boil in a large pot and add the somen noodles. Reduce heat and cook noodles for 3 minutes. Drain.

Serve sautéed tofu over the cooked noodles.

Total calories per serving: 411   Fat: 11 grams   Total Fat as % of Daily Value: 17%
Protein: 21 grams   Iron: 9 mg   Carbohydrates: 59 grams   Calcium: 176 mg
Dietary fiber: 1 grams   Sodium: 227 mg

TOFU CUTLETS
(Serves 4)

This dish has a chewy texture.

1 pound firm tofu, thinly sliced into 12 pieces
2 teaspoons oil
1 Tablespoon tamari or soy sauce
2 Tablespoons water
1/2 cup nutritional yeast
1/4 teaspoon Cajun seasoning
1/4 teaspoon garlic powder

Mix tamari or soy sauce with water in a small bowl. Mix yeast and seasonings together in another small bowl.

Heat oil in a large frying pan over medium heat. Dip slices of tofu in the tamari or soy sauce mixture. Next dip in dish containing yeast and seasonings and cover well. Lay tofu slices in a frying pan and fry for 5 minutes on each side. Serve warm as is or on your favorite whole grain bread with lettuce and sliced tomatoes.

Total calories per serving: 214   Fat: 12 grams   Total Fat as % of Daily Value: 18%
Protein: 23 grams   Iron: 12 mg   Carbohydrates: 9 grams   Calcium: 240 mg
Dietary fiber: 1 gram   Sodium: 268 mg

TOFU AND SCALLIONS WITH CELLOPHANE NOODLES

(Serves 4)

Enjoy this quick and easy main dish.

3-3/4-ounce package cellophane noodles (bean threads)
5 cups boiling water
1 pound tofu, chopped into 1-inch cubes
3 scallions (onion and green tops), finely chopped
1-1/2 teaspoons oil
1/2 teaspoon coriander
1/4 teaspoon cumin
1/4 teaspoon ginger powder
2 teaspoons tamari or soy sauce

Soak noodles in a bowl containing the boiling water for 10 minutes. Drain noodles and chop them into bite-size pieces.

Sauté tofu and scallions in oil in a non-stick frying pan over medium heat for 5 minutes. Add seasonings, tamari, and cooked cellophane noodles. Sauté 1 minute longer. Serve warm.

Total calories per serving: 213   Fat: 7 grams   Total Fat as % of Daily Value: 11%
Protein: 12 grams   Iron: 7 mg   Carbohydrates: 28 grams   Calcium: 124 mg
Dietary fiber: 1 grams   Sodium: 180 mg

TOMATO/BEAN CURD/ SPINACH SAUTÉ

(Serves 3)

If you prefer a spicy dish, simply add more cayenne pepper.

10.5-ounce package lite firm tofu, cubed
10-ounce box frozen spinach, partially thawed
2 medium tomatoes, finely chopped
1/2 cup vegetable broth
2 Tablespoons lemon juice
1/8 teaspoon cayenne

Sauté all the ingredients in a large frying pan over medium-high heat for 15 minutes. Serve warm.

Total calories per serving: 84   Fat: 2 grams   Total Fat as % of Daily Value: 3%
Protein: 9 grams   Iron: 2 mg   Carbohydrates: 11 grams   Calcium: 163 mg
Dietary fiber: 3 grams   Sodium: 235 mg

Main Dishes Made from Other Meat Alternatives:

HEARTY PASTA DISH
(Serves 5)

This dish is very filling.

1 pound pasta (shells, elbows, for example)
5 quarts water
14-ounce package vegan chopped meat alternative (*Gimme Lean, Ground Meatless*, for example)
Small onion, finely chopped
2 teaspoons oil
10-ounce box frozen peas

Cook pasta in boiling water in a large pot until done. Drain.

Sauté the vegan ground meat alternative and onion in the oil in a large non-stick frying pan over medium heat for 5 minutes. Chop up the browned mixture and add the peas. Stir in the cooked pasta and mix well. Serve warm.

Total calories per serving: 402 Fat: 3 grams Total Fat as % of Daily Value: 5%
Protein: 15 grams Iron: 5 mg Carbohydrates: 77 grams Calcium: 33 mg
Dietary fiber: 5 grams Sodium: 56 mg

HEARTY SKILLET DISH

(Serves 5)

A colorful, hearty main dish that can be served over rice.

14-ounce package vegan chopped meat alternative (*Gimme Lean, Ground Meatless*, for example)
Small onion, finely chopped
1 Tablespoon oil
10-ounce box frozen peas
1/2 teaspoon oregano
14-ounce can diced tomatoes in juice or whole tomatoes, chopped, (keep juice)

Sauté the vegan ground meat alternative and onion in the oil in a large non-stick frying pan over medium-high heat for 10 minutes. While cooking chop up the "meat." Add the peas and oregano and sauté for 3 minutes. Last, add the tomatoes with liquid and simmer 3 more minutes. Serve warm.

Total calories per serving: 188   Fat: 3 grams   Total Fat as % of Daily Value: 5%
Protein: 16 grams   Iron: 2 mg   Carbohydrates: 24 grams   Calcium: 37 mg
Dietary fiber: 4 grams   Sodium: 515 mg

'HOT DOGS' AND BEANS CASSEROLE

(Serves 4)

Here's a quick and easy dish to prepare.

8 vegan fat-free hot dogs, sliced into thin rounds
15-ounce can navy or great northern beans, rinsed and
    drained
15-ounce can kidney or pinto beans, rinsed and drained
15-ounce can no salt added tomato sauce
1/4 cup molasses

Preheat oven to 350 degrees. Meanwhile, mix all the ingredients together and pour into a 2-quart glass baking dish. Bake for 30 minutes at 350 degrees. Remove from oven and serve warm.

Total calories per serving: 387   Fat: 1 gram   Total Fat as % of Daily Value: 2%
Protein: 33 grams   Iron: 8 mg   Carbohydrates: 60 grams   Calcium: 194 mg
Dietary fiber: 7 grams   Sodium: 886 mg

'HOT DOGS,' PEPPERS, AND ONION

(Serves 4)

This dish is quite simple to prepare.

8 vegan hot dogs, sliced into 1-inch wide pieces
1 green bell pepper — cored, seeded, and finely chopped
1 red bell pepper — cored, seeded, and finely chopped
Small onion, finely chopped
2 teaspoons oil
2 Tablespoons prepared mustard (spicy yellow is best)

Sauté all the ingredients except the mustard in a large non-stick frying pan over medium heat for 8 minutes. Add mustard and sauté another 2 minutes. Serve warm.

Total calories per serving: 163   Fat: 8 grams   Total Fat as % of Daily Value: 12%
Protein: 17 grams   Iron: 4 mg   Carbohydrates: 8 grams   Calcium: 54 mg
Dietary fiber: 1 gram   Sodium: 378 mg

LAYERED NOODLE DISH

(Serves 4)

This dish takes a little extra time to prepare but is well worth the effort.

1 pound lasagna noodles
5 quarts water
8-ounce package frozen vegan 'sausage' patties or links,
  partially thawed and cubed
1 pound eggplant, peeled and cubed
Small onion, finely chopped
1 cup vegetable broth
Two 15-ounce cans tomato sauce

Cook noodles in boiling water for 10 minutes until tender. Drain.

Meanwhile, sauté vegan 'sausage' patties or links, eggplant, and onion in broth in a large pot over medium heat for 15 minutes.

Preheat oven to 350 degrees. In a 13"x9"x2" pan place the following layers: half a 15-ounce can of sauce, 1/3 of the cooked noodles, 1/2 of the cooked eggplant/sausage/onion mixture. Repeat layers twice. Then follow with half a 15-ounce can of sauce, 1/3 of the noodles, and half a 15-ounce can of sauce. Bake 20 minutes at 350 degrees. Serve warm with a green salad.

Total calories per serving: 656   Fat: 8 grams   Total Fat as % of Daily Value: 12%
Protein: 29 grams   Iron: 10 mg   Carbohydrates: 121 grams   Calcium: 142 mg
Dietary fiber: 6 grams   Sodium: 1668 mg

SAUTÉED 'SAUSAGE' OVER MASHED POTATOES

(Serves 4)

If asparagus is not in season, you may substitute chopped celery.

8 medium white potatoes, peeled and chopped
6 cups water
8-ounce package vegan sausage patties or links, partially
    thawed and cubed
1 pound asparagus, chopped
2 teaspoons oil
15-ounce can tomato sauce

Bring water to a boil in a large pot. Add potatoes, reduce heat and cook potatoes until tender. Drain and mash potatoes.

    Meanwhile, sauté vegan 'sausage' patties or links and asparagus in oil in a large frying pan over medium-high heat for 8 minutes. Add sauce, reduce heat, and simmer 2 more minutes. Serve sauce mixture over mashed potatoes.

Total calories per serving: 445   Fat: 8 grams   Total Fat as % of Daily Value: 12%
Protein: 21 grams   Iron: 6 mg   Carbohydrates: 76 grams   Calcium: 130 mg
Dietary fiber: 7 grams   Sodium: 936 mg

STUFFED PEPPERS

(Serves 4)

Your guests will never believe that these peppers
are stuffed without animal products.

4 large green bell peppers, tops sliced off and seeds removed
2 teaspoons oil
Small onion finely chopped
14-ounce package vegan ground meat (*Gimme Lean!
Sausage Flavor, Ground Meatless*, for example)
2 medium ripe tomatoes, finely chopped

Bring a large pot of water to a boil. Submerge cleaned-out peppers in
boiling water and boil for 10 minutes. Carefully remove peppers and
drain.

In a large frying pan, heat oil and sauté onion and vegan ground meat
alternative for 4 minutes over medium-high heat, chopping up mixture
once in a while. Add tomato and stir mixture one minute longer.

Stuff peppers with mixture and serve immediately.

Total calories per serving: 187   Fat: 3 grams   Total Fat as % of Daily Value: 5%
Protein: 18 grams   Iron: 1 mg   Carbohydrates: 24 grams   Calcium: 15 mg
Dietary fiber: 3 grams   Sodium: 516 mg

Side Dishes Made From Meat Alternatives:

BAKED LIMA BEANS

(Serves 8)

This sweet side dish is absolutely delicious!

6-ounce package vegan 'bacon'
2 teaspoons oil
24-ounce package frozen lima beans
1/2 small onion, finely chopped
6-ounce can tomato sauce
1/2 cup molasses
2 Tablespoons nutritional yeast

Fry vegan 'bacon' in oil in a non-stick frying pan until crisp on both sides (about 10 minutes). Chop into very small pieces.

Preheat oven to 350 degrees. Cook lima beans in boiling water for 10 minutes and drain.

Mix all the ingredients together and pour into a medium-size oven-proof covered baking dish. Bake 30 minutes at 350 degrees. Serve warm.

Total calories per serving: 185   Fat: 2 grams   Total Fat as % of Daily Value: 3%
Protein: 9 grams   Iron: 3 mg   Carbohydrates: 33 grams   Calcium: 118 mg
Dietary fiber: 5 grams   Sodium: 278 mg

SEITAN/POTATO KNISHES

(Makes 12)

*These delicious knishes (potato-stuffed pocket sandwiches)
make a terrific lunch or snack.*

3 pounds white potatoes (4 large), peeled and chopped
4 cups water
Medium onion, finely chopped
8-ounce package seitan, drained and finely cubed
2 teaspoons oil
1 teaspoon turmeric
Salt and pepper to taste
3 cups unbleached white flour
2 teaspoons baking powder

Cook potatoes in boiling water in a medium-size pot for about 20
minutes or until tender. Drain.

Sauté onion and seitan in oil in a non-stick frying pan over medium-
high heat for 5 minutes.

Mash cooked potatoes and divide mixture in half. Stir half the mashed
potatoes with the sautéed seitan/onion mixture. Mix the remaining
mashed potatoes with the turmeric, salt and pepper, flour, and baking
powder to create a dough. Knead dough for a few minutes. Then, roll
dough out on a floured surface until 1/4-inch thick. Cut dough into
twelve 4" x 4" squares. Place 1/12th of potato/seitan/onion mixture on
each square. Fold corners of dough in and pinch dough tight in center.

Preheat oven to 375 degrees. Place knishes (pinched side down) on
lightly oiled cookie sheet. Bake at 375 degrees for 45 minutes. Serve
warm with mustard.

Total calories per knish: 226   Fat: 1 gram   Total Fat as % of Daily Value: 2%
Protein: 8 grams   Iron: 2 mg   Carbohydrates: 45 grams   Calcium: 59 mg
Dietary fiber: 3 grams   Sodium: 188 mg

TOFU, KALE, AND RAISINS

(Serves 4)

This is a quick-and-easy side dish.
Feel free to substitute different dark leafy greens, dried fruit, and/or juice.

1 pound tofu, drained and chopped into 1-inch cubes
4 cups (about 1/2 pound) finely shredded kale
1 cup raisins
1/2 teaspoon coriander
1/2 cup orange juice

Sauté ingredients in a large non-stick frying pan over medium heat for 8 minutes. Serve warm.

Total calories per serving: 214   Fat: 6 grams   Total Fat as % of Daily Value: 9%
Protein: 11 grams   Iron: 7 mg   Carbohydrates: 35 grams   Calcium: 151 mg
Dietary fiber: 2 grams   Sodium: 17 mg

TOFU/POTATO PANCAKES

(Makes 8 pancakes -- serve 2 per person)

These pancakes are delicate and fluffy.
They can be served at Chanukah and year-round with applesauce.

2 pounds white potatoes, peeled and chopped
6 cups water
10.5-ounce package extra firm lite tofu, crumbled
1/2 cup matzo meal
Small onion, finely chopped
1/4 teaspoon dill weed
Salt and pepper to taste
2 Tablespoons oil (for pan)

Place potatoes and water in a large covered pot. Bring to a boil, reduce heat and cook 15 minutes over a medium-high heat. Drain.

Place the cooked potatoes and remaining ingredients (except oil) in a food processor cup. Blend until smooth (about 3 minutes). You may have to stop and scrape the sides of the food processor cup once or twice.

Heat oil in a large non-stick frying pan over medium-high heat. Brown pancakes on each side for 8 minutes. Flip over carefully. Serve warm pancakes with applesauce.

Total calories per serving (without applesauce): 342   Fat: 8 grams
Total Fat as % of Daily Value: 12%   Protein: 12 grams   Iron: 3 mg
Carbohydrates: 57 grams   Calcium: 42 mg   Dietary fiber: 4 grams   Sodium: 85 mg

BEVERAGES

SPARKLING APPLE DELIGHT

(Serves 4)

Enjoy this unique beverage.

Large bottle chilled sparkling cider (about 25 ounces)
1 large apple — peeled, cored, and finely grated
1/4 teaspoon ginger powder

Stir all the ingredients together in a large pitcher. Serve immediately.

Total calories per serving: 106   Fat: <1 gram   Total Fat as % of Daily Value: <1%
Protein:<1 gram   Iron: <1 mg   Carbohydrates: 27 grams   Calcium: 2 mg
Dietary fiber: 1 gram   Sodium: 27 mg

CHOCOLATE SHAKE

(Serves 2)

This beverage is terrific for a snack and quite filling.

2 Tablespoons cocoa powder
2 ripe bananas, peeled
2-1/2 cups chilled lite soy milk or other milk alternative
3 Tablespoons maple syrup

Blend all the ingredients together in a blender cup for 1 minute and serve.

Total calories per serving: 300   Fat: 3 grams   Total Fat as % of Daily Value: 5%
Protein: 6 grams   Iron: 3 mg   Carbohydrates: 68 grams   Calcium: 145 mg
Dietary fiber: 3 grams   Sodium: 126 mg

SPICED WHITE GRAPE JUICE

(Serves 4)

Here's a warm beverage.

6 cups white grape juice
1-1/2 teaspoons cinnamon
1/2 teaspoon clove powder

Heat all the ingredients in a large pot over medium heat for 5 minutes. Stir while heating. Serve warm in 4 mugs.

Total calories per serving: 188   Fat: <1 gram   Total Fat as % of Daily Value: <1%
Protein: 1 gram   Iron: <1 mg   Carbohydrates: 47 grams   Calcium: 15 mg
Dietary fiber: <1 gram   Sodium: 7 mg

SOOTHING ORANGE JUICE

(Serves 3)

Serve this hot beverage on a cold winter night!

3 cups orange juice
1 juice orange — peeled, thinly sliced, and seeds removed
1/8 teaspoon cinnamon
1/8 teaspoon clove powder

Heat all the ingredients in a medium-size pot over medium heat for 10 minutes. Serve warm in 3 mugs.

Total calories per serving: 132   Fat: <1 gram   Total Fat as % of Daily Value: <1%
Protein: 2 grams   Iron: <1 mg   Carbohydrates: 32 grams   Calcium: 41 mg
Dietary fiber: 1 gram   Sodium: 2 mg

STRAWBERRY/BANANA SHAKE

(Serves 3)

Enjoy this refreshing thick shake.

2 cups lite soy milk or other milk alternative
2 ripe bananas, peeled
1 cup strawberries (about 8-9 large), stems removed

Place all the ingredients in a blender cup and blend at high speed for 2 minutes. Serve in three glasses.

Total calories per serving: 145   Fat: 2 grams   Total Fat as % of Daily Value: 3%
Protein: 3 grams   Iron: <1 mg   Carbohydrates: 32 grams   Calcium: 38 mg
Dietary fiber: 3 grams   Sodium: 64 mg

BREAKFASTS

AMARANTH AND PEACHES
(Serves 6)

Amaranth is a grain that can be found in natural foods stores and gourmet shops. Three fresh peaches can be substituted for the canned peaches.

2 cups amaranth
4 cups water
1/2 cup raisins
16-ounce can peaches in own juice, drained, and chopped
1/2 teaspoon cinnamon
1/4 cup maple syrup

Bring amaranth and water to a boil in a medium-size pot. Reduce heat to medium and cook covered for 25 minutes.

Add raisins, peaches, cinnamon, and maple syrup. Cook another 5 minutes. Serve warm.

Total calories per serving: 345 Fat: 4 grams Total Fat as % of Daily Value: 6%
Protein: 10 grams Iron: 6 mg Carbohydrates: 70 grams Calcium: 123 mg
Dietary fiber: 2 grams Sodium: 20 mg

APPLE POCKETS

(Serves 5)

Children and adults alike will enjoy this dish.
Substitute pears or peaches for variety.

4 apples — peeled, cored, and chopped
2 Tablespoons apple juice
1/2 teaspoon cinnamon
1 Tablespoon maple syrup
5 medium whole wheat pita breads

Heat apples, juice, cinnamon, and syrup in a medium-size pot over medium-high heat for 5 minutes. Stir occasionally.

Cut pitas in half cross-wise to form 2 pockets. Spoon apple mixture into each half. Warm apple pockets up in a toaster oven or oven at 350 degrees for 3 minutes before serving.

Total calories per serving: 241   Fat: 2 grams   Total Fat as % of Daily Value: 3%
Protein: 6 grams   Iron: <1 mg   Carbohydrates: 54 grams   Calcium: 18 mg
Dietary fiber: 2 grams   Sodium: 341 mg

BANANA BISCUITS

(Makes 35)

These delicious biscuits make a perfect breakfast item.
Leftovers can be reheated in a toaster oven the next day.

3 small ripe bananas, peeled and mashed
1 cup lite soy milk or other milk alternative
2 Tablespoons oil
4-1/4 cups unbleached white flour
1 Tablespoon baking powder

Preheat oven to 425 degrees. Mix the mashed bananas, soy milk, and oil together in a large bowl. Add the flour and baking powder and stir well.

Place dough on a floured surface and knead for 3 minutes. Using a rolling pin, roll dough to a 3/4-inch thickness. Cut into 2-inch wide circles using a cutter or tin can. Place biscuits on a lightly oiled cookie sheet. Bake 20 minutes at 425 degrees until browned. Serve warm.

Total calories per biscuit: 72   Fat: 1 gram   Total Fat as % of Daily Value: 2%
Protein: 2 grams   Iron: 1 mg   Carbohydrates: 14 grams   Calcium: 28 mg
Dietary fiber: 1 gram   Sodium: 45 mg

YUMMY FRENCH TOAST

(Serves 4 -- 2 slices per person)

A delicious batter makes this French toast irresistible.

16-ounce can fruit (peaches or pears), keep juice
1/2 cup soy or rice milk
1/8 teaspoon cinnamon
8 slices whole grain bread

Blend fruit, soy or rice milk, and cinnamon together in a blender until smooth. Soak slices of bread in mixture and fry 5 minutes on each side in a lightly oiled frying pan over medium heat. Serve warm.

Total calories per serving: 241   Fat: 6 grams   Total Fat as % of Daily Value: 9%
Protein: 7 grams   Iron: 2 mg   Carbohydrates: 43 grams   Calcium: 59 mg
Dietary fiber: 1 gram   Sodium: 315 mg

MANDARIN PANCAKES

(Makes 5 large or 10 small pancakes)

Enjoy these uniquely flavored pancakes.

2 cups unbleached white flour
1 Tablespoon Egg Replacer (Ener-G, for example)
2 teaspoons baking powder
10.5-ounce can mandarin oranges, including juice
1 cup water

Mix the ingredients together in a medium-size bowl. Pour batter into a lightly oiled non-stick frying pan. Cook pancakes over medium heat for 5 minutes on each side. Serve warm.

Total calories per large pancake: 211   Fat: <1 gram   Total Fat as % of Daily Value: <1%
Protein: 6 grams   Iron: 2 mg   Carbohydrates: 46 grams   Calcium: 146 mg
Dietary fiber: 2 grams   Sodium: 199 mg

QUINOA AND PINEAPPLE CEREAL

(Serves 4)

Feel free to substitute your favorite chopped fruit for the pineapple.

1 cup quinoa (about half a 12-ounce box)
2 cups water
1/2 teaspoon cinnamon
20-ounce can pineapple chunks, drained or 1-1/2 cups fresh
  pineapple chunks

Cook quinoa with water and cinnamon in a medium-size pot over medium heat for 15 minutes. Remove from stove and toss in pineapple. Serve warm. Chilled leftovers are also delicious!

Total calories per serving: 215   Fat: 3 grams   Total Fat as % of Daily Value: 5%
Protein: 6 grams   Iron: 4 mg   Carbohydrates: 44 grams   Calcium: 38 mg
Dietary fiber: 3 grams   Sodium: 10 mg

LUNCHES OR SNACKS

BEAN BURGERS

(Makes 4 burgers)

*Serve these burgers with your favorite gravy or
on a whole wheat bun with lettuce and tomato.*

19-ounce can white kidney (cannellini) beans — rinsed,
  drained, and mashed
2 scallions, finely chopped (bulb and green stems)
1 Tablespoon vegan 'bacon' bits (*Fakin' Bacon Bits*, for
  example)
Pepper to taste
1/4 cup whole wheat pastry flour

Place all the ingredients in a medium-size bowl and mix well. Form 4
burgers and fry on each side for 8 minutes in a lightly oiled frying pan
over medium heat. Serve warm.

Total calories per burger: 135   Fat: 1 gram   Total Fat as % of Daily Value: 2%
Protein: 7 grams   Iron: 2 mg   Carbohydrates: 24 grams   Calcium: 44 mg
Dietary fiber: 6 grams   Sodium: 290 mg

SQUASH CORN MUFFINS

(Makes 18 large muffins)

These hearty muffins are terrific to eat on the go.

1-1/2 cups cornmeal
1-1/2 cups unbleached white flour
1 Tablespoon plus 1 teaspoon baking powder
2 teaspoons baking soda
1-1/2 pounds zucchini or yellow squash, grated
10-ounce box frozen corn kernels, partially thawed
1 teaspoon basil
1/2 cup molasses or other liquid sweetener
1-1/2 cups water

Preheat oven to 375 degrees.

    Mix all the ingredients together in a large mixing bowl. Pour batter into 18 lightly oiled muffin cups. Bake muffins for 25 minutes at 375 degrees. Allow to cool before removing from tins.

Total calories per muffin: 123   Fat: 1 grams   Total Fat as % of Daily Value: 2%
Protein: 3 grams   Iron: 1 mg   Carbohydrates: 24 grams   Calcium: 95 mg
Dietary fiber: 2 grams   Sodium: 254 mg

PITA BREAD PIZZA

(Serves 6)

Kids will enjoy this dish since they can choose their own favorite toppings.

Six 6-inch round whole wheat pita breads
16-ounce jar vegan pasta sauce
3 cups chopped vegetables (onions, mushrooms, spinach,
tomatoes, green peppers, for example)

Place 1/6 of the pasta sauce on top of each pita bread. Lay 1/2 cup of mixed chopped vegetables on top of the sauce on each pizza.

Place pizza under a broiler in the oven for about 3 minutes until warm. Serve immediately.

Total calories per serving: 265   Fat: 4 grams   Total Fat as % of Daily Value: 6%
Protein: 8 grams   Iron: 1 mg   Carbohydrates: 50 grams   Calcium: 54 mg
Dietary fiber: 2 grams   Sodium: 688 mg

LIMA BEAN SPREAD

(Makes about 1-1/2 cups -- 3 servings)

This thick bean spread is simple to prepare and quite filling.

10-ounce box frozen lima beans
1 cup water
2 Tablespoons lemon juice
1 teaspoon marjoram

Bring water to a boil in a small pot. Add lima beans and continue cooking 15 minutes over medium-high heat. Drain off excess liquid.

Pour cooked lima beans into a food processor cup. Add remaining ingredients and blend until creamy. Refrigerate at least 1 hour before serving on your favorite whole grain bread or with crackers.

Total calories per 1/2 cup serving: 97   Fat: <1 gram   Total Fat as % of Daily Value: <1%
Protein: 6 grams   Iron: 1 mg   Carbohydrates: 18 grams   Calcium: 22 mg
Dietary fiber: 5 grams   Sodium: 55 mg

TOFU/PIMENTO SPREAD
(Makes about 1-1/2 cups -- 6 servings)

Serve this sandwich spread on a whole grain bread with lettuce and tomato.

1 pound tofu, drained and crumbled
2-ounce jar pimentos
1/4 cup nutritional yeast
1-1/2 Tablespoons prepared mustard

Place all the ingredients in a food processor cup and blend until creamy. The spread can be served right away or chilled before serving.

Total calories per 1/4 cup serving: 73   Fat: 4 grams   Total Fat as % of Daily Value: 6%
Protein: 8 grams   Iron: 4 mg   Carbohydrates: 3 grams   Calcium: 85 mg
Dietary fiber: <1 grams   Sodium: 58 mg

DESSERTS

BANANA/OATMEAL/COCONUT BAR COOKIES

(Makes 16)

This dessert is simple to prepare.

2 large ripe bananas, peeled and mashed
2 cups quick rolled oats
1 cup shredded coconut
1/4 cup maple syrup or other liquid sweetner

Preheat oven to 350 degrees. Mix ingredients together in a large bowl. Flatten dough in a 9"x9"x2" non-stick baking pan. Bake for 30 minutes. Cool pan on a wire rack when removed from oven. Once cool, slice into 16 square cookies and serve.

Total calories per cookie: 77   Fat: 2 grams   Total Fat as % of Daily Value: 3%
Protein: 1 gram   Iron: <1 mg   Carbohydrates: 13 grams   Calcium: 10 mg
Dietary fiber: 1 gram   Sodium: 16 mg

BREAD PUDDING

(Serves 6)

This dessert tastes fantastic!

3 cups vanilla-flavored soy milk or other milk alternative
5 Tablespoons cornstarch
1/2 cup maple syrup
6 slices whole grain bread, chopped into 1-inch cubes
1/4 teaspoon cinnamon

Place the soy milk, cornstarch, and syrup in a medium-size pot. Mix with a whisk for a minute. Add the whole grain bread and cinnamon and heat over medium-high heat until pudding starts to thicken. Remove from stove and pour into 6 dessert bowls or one 9"x9"x2" pan. Place in the refrigerator and chill for at least one hour before serving.

Total calories per serving: 245   Fat: 4 grams   Total Fat as % of Daily Value: 6%
Protein: 6 grams   Iron: 2 mg   Carbohydrates: 49 grams   Calcium: 97 mg
Dietary fiber: 1 gram   Sodium: 200 mg

CHOCOLATE PIE

(Serves 8)

This pie is guaranteed to be a crowd-pleaser at any gathering.

3 cups lite soy milk or other milk alternative
1/2 cup maple syrup
1/2 cup unsweetened cocoa powder or carob powder
1/4 cup cornstarch
9-inch pre-made lowfat vegan Graham Cracker-style pie shell

Place the soymilk, syrup, cocoa, and cornstarch in a medium-size pot over medium-high heat. Mix with a whisk constantly until the mixture starts to bubble. Reduce heat and stir until the pudding thickens (about 1 minute). Remove from the stove and pour into the pie crust. Refrigerate at least one hour before serving.

Total calories per serving: 191   Fat: 3 grams   Total Fat as % of Daily Value: 5%
Protein: 2 grams   Iron: 3 mg   Carbohydrates: 41 grams   Calcium: 64 mg
Dietary fiber: <1 grams   Sodium: 139 mg

CORN PUDDING

(Serves 4)

Serve this unique pudding with a dash of cinnamon.

15-ounce can vegan cream-style corn
1 cup soy milk or other milk alternative
1/4 cup cornstarch
1/2 teaspoon vanilla
1/2 cup maple syrup

Cook all the ingredients together in a medium-size pot over medium-high heat, stirring often, until mixture begins to boil and thicken. Once thick, remove pudding from heat and pour into four dessert-size dishes. Chill at least 30 minutes before serving.

Total calories per serving: 246   Fat: 2 grams   Total Fat as % of Daily Value: 3%
Protein: 3 grams   Iron: 1 mg   Carbohydrates: 58 grams   Calcium: 68 mg
Dietary fiber: 2 grams   Sodium: 332 mg

COUSCOUS PUDDING

(Serves 4)

Experiment with different types of dried fruit for variety.

5 ounces couscous (a little less than 1 cup)
1/2 cup dried fruit (raisins, chopped figs or dates, for
    example)
1-1/2 cups water
1-1/2 cups soy milk or other milk alternative
1/4 cup maple syrup
1/4 teaspoon cinnamon
2 Tablespoons cornstarch

Bring water to a boil in a small pot. Add couscous and dried fruit. Cover pot, remove from heat, and allow to sit 5 minutes.

    Meanwhile, in a medium-size pot, heat remaining ingredients over medium-high heat until the pudding starts to thicken (about 3 minutes). While heating, stir often with a whisk. Once pudding thickens, remove from heat, and add cooked couscous mixture. Mix well. Pour pudding into a serving dish and chill for at least 1 hour before serving.

Total calories per serving: 319   Fat: 2 grams   Total Fat as % of Daily Value: 3%
Protein: 7 grams   Iron: 1 mg   Carbohydrates: 69 grams   Calcium: 74 mg
Dietary fiber: 7 grams   Sodium: 43 mg

FRUIT PIZZA

(Serves 4)

Here's a beautiful looking dessert that both children and adults will enjoy. You can also substitute several small pita breads for the large pita bread.

1 large 12-inch wide pita bread
1 cup unsweetened apple butter
1 kiwi, peeled and sliced
6 large strawberries, sliced
1 apple or pear — peeled, cored, and thinly sliced
1/4 teaspoon cinnamon

Spread apple butter over pita bread. Arrange slices of fruit on top of apple butter. Sprinkle with cinnamon. Serve as is or heat in 350 degree oven for 15 minutes and serve warm.

Total calories per serving: 269   Fat: 1 gram   Total Fat as % of Daily Value: 2%
Protein: 4 grams   Iron: 1 mg   Carbohydrates: 48 grams   Calcium: 48 mg
Dietary fiber: 2 grams   Sodium: 162 mg

SOURCES OF VEGAN PRODUCTS

The following is a list of suppliers of various vegan products used in this cookbook. Please note that other supermarket chains may have other brands not listed here. Also, in some cases I have indicated that we are listing organic brands only now that they are widely distributed. If you are unable to locate certain foods when you shop, I encourage you to show this list to the store manager or buyer and encourage him or her to stock these items. Don't forget that some items can also be purchased from bins in bulk or frozen in the freezer case.

GRAINS

Amaranth:
> Arrowhead Mills, Hereford, TX
> Bread and Circus, Fresh Fields, and Whole Foods distributed by
> Whole Foods Inc., Austin, TX
> Nu-World Amaranth, Naperville, IL

Barley:
> Arrowhead Mills, Hereford, TX
> Bread and Circus, Fresh Fields, and Whole Foods distributed by
> Whole Foods Inc., Austin, TX
> Goya Foods, Inc., Secaucus, NJ
> Quaker Foods Co., Chicago, IL

Basmati Rice:

American Roland Food Corp., New York, NY
Asian Brand, Inc., Norwalk, CA
Bread and Circus, Fresh Fields, and Whole Foods distributed by
    Whole Foods Inc., Austin, TX
Fantastic Foods, Petaluma, CA
Kasmati Indian-Style Basmati from RiceTec, Inc., Alvin, TX
Kusha, Inc., Rolling Hills, CA
Lundberg Family Farms, Richdale, CA
Master Choice distributed by Compass Foods, Montvale, NJ
Texmati Long Grain Basmati from RiceTec, Inc., Alvin, TX
Tilda Basmati Rice from Tilda Marketing Inc., Englewoods Cliffs,
    NJ

Bread Crumbs (Beware most packaged varieties are not vegan):

Giant Food Inc., Landover, MD
Jason Foods Inc., Elmwood Park, NJ

Bulgur:

American Roland Food Corp., New York, NY
Bread and Circus, Fresh Fields, and Whole Foods distributed by
    Whole Foods Inc., Austin, TX
Oldworld from Ener-G Foods, Inc., Seattle, WA
Sovex Natural Foods, Inc., Collegedale, TN

Couscous:

American Roland Food Corp., New York, NY
Arrowhead Mills, Hereford, TX
Bread and Circus, Fresh Fields, and Whole Foods distributed by
    Whole Foods Inc., Austin, TX
Casabah/Sahara Natural Foods, San Leandro, CA
Fantastic Foods, Petaluma, CA
Master Choice distributed by Compass Foods, Montvale, NJ
Near East Couscous Moroccan Pasta, Leominster, MA
Osem Israeli Toasted Couscous from Nakid Ltd., Tel Aviv, Israel

Farfel:

Osem Israeli Haimishe Farfel from Nakid Ltd., Tel Aviv, Israel

Matzo Meal:
>Aaron Streit Inc., New York, NY
>The B. Manischewitz Co., Jersey City, NJ
>Horowitz Margareten distributed by GMB Enterprises, Inc., Jersey City, NJ

Millet:
>Arrowhead Mills, Hereford, TX
>Bread and Circus, Fresh Fields, and Whole Foods distributed by Whole Foods Inc., Austin, TX

Oriental Cellophane Noodles (Bean Threads):
>China Bowl Trading Co., Westport, CT
>Kame distributed by Shaffer, Clarke & Co., Inc., Darien, CT
>Port Arthur Gourmet Award Foods, St. Paul, MN
>Sun Luck distributed by Seasia, Seattle, WA

Quinoa:
>Ancient Harvest distributed by Quinoa Corp., Torrance, CA
>Arrowhead Mills, Hereford, TX
>Bread and Circus, Fresh Fields, and Whole Foods distributed by Whole Foods Inc., Austin, TX

Somen Noodles:
>Kame distributed by Shaffer, Clarke & Co., Inc., Darien, CT

Udon Noodles:
>Eden Foods, Inc., Clinton, MI
>Sobaya, Canada

Wild Rice:
>American Roland Food Corp., New York, NY
>Bread and Circus, Fresh Fields, and Whole Foods distributed by Whole Foods Inc., Austin, TX
>Grey Owl Foods, Grand Rapids, MN
>Mac Dougall's, Marysville, CA
>Mille Lacs M.P., Company, Madison, WI

LEGUMES

Canned Black Beans:
American Prairie distributed by Mercantile Food Co., Philmont, NY
Diana Foods, Inc., Miami, FL
Eden Foods, Inc., Clinton, MI
Goya Foods, Inc., Secaucus, NJ
Green Giant Pillsbury Co., Minneapolis, MN
Progresso Quality Foods Co., St. Louis, MO
Walnut Acres, Penns Creek, PA
Westbrae Natural Foods, Carson, CA

Canned Black-Eyed Peas:
American Prairie distributed by Mercantile Food Co., Philmont, NY
Goya Foods, Inc., Secaucus, NJ
Hanover Foods Corp., Hanover, PA

Canned Chickpeas (Garbanzo Beans, Ceci Beans):
American Prairie distributed by Mercantile Food Co., Philmont, NY
America's Choice distributed by Compass Foods, Montvale, NJ
Cento Fine Foods, Inc., Thorofare, NJ
Diana Foods, Inc., Miami, FL
Eden Foods, Inc., Clinton, MI
Fuhrman Foods, Inc., Northumberland, PA
Goya Foods, Inc., Secaucus, NJ
Hain Pure Foods, Uniondale, NY
Hanover Foods Corp., Hanover, PA
Progresso Quality Foods Co., St. Louis, MO
Sclafani distributed by Gus Sclafani Corp., Stanford, CT
Super G from Giant Supermarkets, Landover, MD
Unger's distributed by Quality Frozen Foods, Inc., Brooklyn, NY
Walnut Acres, Penns Creek, PA
Westbrae Natural Foods, Carson, CA

Canned Fava Beans
Alreef, Inc., Detroit, MI
Mira Int'l Foods, Milltown, NJ
Progresso Quality Foods Co., St. Louis, MO

Canned Kidney Beans (Red and Cannellini):
American Prairie distributed by Mercantile Food Co., Philmont,
    NY
America's Choice distributed by Compass Foods, Montvale, NJ
Cento Fine Foods, Inc., Thorofare, NJ
Eden Foods, Inc., Clinton, MI
Goya Foods, Inc., Secaucus, NJ
Haddar distributed by Ebba Food Products, Inc., Brooklyn, NY
Hanover Foods Corp., Hanover, PA
The Pastene Companies, Ltd., Waltham, MA
Pastore Inc., Baltimore, MD
Progresso Quality Foods Co., St. Louis, MO
Sclafani distributed by Gus Sclafani Corp., Stanford, CT
Super G from Giant Supermarkets, Landover, MD
Unger's distributed by Quality Frozen Foods, Inc., Brooklyn, NY
Walnut Acres, Penns Creek, PA
Westbrae Natural Foods, Carson, CA

Canned Pinto Beans:
American Prairie distributed by Mercantile Food Co., Philmont,
    NY
Bush Brothers and Company, Knoxville, TN
Eden Foods, Inc., Clinton, MI
Goya Foods, Inc., Secaucus, NJ
Hain Pure Foods, Uniondale, NY
Progresso Quality Foods Co., St. Louis, MO
Walnut Acres, Penns Creek, PA
Westbrae Natural Foods, Carson, CA

Dried Red Lentils:
Arrowhead Mills, Hereford, TX
Bread and Circus, Fresh Fields, and Whole Foods distributed by
    Whole Foods Inc., Austin, TX

Refried Beans: See Mexican Products

Canned White Beans (Navy, Great Northern, etc.):
American Prairie distributed by Mercantile Food Co., Philmont, NY
America's Choice distributed by Compass Foods, Montvale, NJ
Eden Foods, Inc., Clinton, MI
Fuhrman Foods, Inc., Northumberland, PA
Goya Foods, Inc., Secaucus, NJ
Hanover Foods Corp., Hanover, PA
Westbrae Natural Foods, Carson, CA

Dried Yellow Split Peas:
American Roland Food Corp., New York, NY
Bread and Circus, Fresh Fields, and Whole Foods distributed by Whole Foods Inc., Austin, TX
Goya Foods, Inc., Secaucus, NJ
Martha White Foods, Nashville, TN
Unger's distributed by Quality Frozen Foods, Inc., Brooklyn, NY

MEAT ALTERNATIVES

Vegan 'Bacon':
Canadian Style Veggie Bacon, Stop and Shop, Boston, MA
Fakin' Bacon Bits from Lightlife Foods, Inc., Turner Falls, MA (note Fakin' Bacon has honey, bits do not contain honey)
Yves Canadian Veggie Bacon, from Yves Veggie Cuisine, Inc., Delta (Vancouver), British Columbia, Canada

Chicken-Style Wheat Meat:
Meat of Wheat distributed by White Wave Inc., Boulder, CO

Vegan Ground Meat:

Gimme Lean! from Lightlife Foods, Inc., Turner Falls, MA
Hearty and Natural Classic Meatless Ground Soyburger
distributed by Springhill Farm Foods, Minneapolis, MN
Just Like Ground! from Yves Veggies Cuisine, Inc., Vancouver,
British Columbia, Canada
Morningstar Farms Ground Meatless distributed by Worthington
Foods, Inc., Worthington, OH
Nature's Ground Meatless from Vegenarian, Inc., South San
Francisco, CA
Protein Crumbles distributed by Worthington Foods, Inc.,
Worthington, OH
Vegan Crumbles from Natural Touch and distributed by
Worthington Foods Inc., Worthington, OH

Vegan 'Hot Dogs':

Lightlife Foods, Inc., Turner Falls, MA
Natural Touch from Worthington Foods Inc., Worthington, OH
Northern Soy Inc., New York, NY
Stop and Shop, Boston, MA
Tounatur Foods Inc., Quebec, Canada
Vitasoy Inc., Brisbane, CA
White Wave Inc., Boulder, CO
Wholesome & Hearty, Portland, OR
Yves Veggie Cuisine, Inc., Delta (Vancouver), British Columbia,
Canada

Vegan 'Sausage' Patties or Links:

Lightlife Foods, Inc., Turner Falls, MA
Northern Soy Inc., Rochester, NY
Spring Creek Natural Foods, Spencer, WV
Twin Oaks Community Foods, Louisa, VA
Yves Veggie Cuisine, Inc., Delta (Vancouver), British Columbia,
Canada

Seitan (Wheat Gluten):
Lightlife Foods, Inc., Turner Falls, MA
Tofu Shop Specialty Foods Inc., Arcata, CA
Upcountry, Pittsfield, MA
White Wave Inc., Boulder, CO

Tempeh:
Cricklewood Soyfoods, Mertztown, PA
Lightlife Foods, Inc., Turner Falls, MA
Quong Hop and Co., South San Francisco, CA
Surata Soyfoods Co-op, Eugene, OR
Turtle Island Foods Inc., Hood River, OR
White Wave Inc., Boulder, CO
Wildwood Natural Foods, Fairfax, CA
Yaupon Soyfoods, Elgin, TX

Tofu:
American Soyfoods Industry, Elkridge, MD
Bread and Circus distributed by Whole Foods, Austin, TX
Morinaga Nutritional Foods Inc., Los Angeles, CA
Nasoya Foods Inc., Leominster, MA
Northern Soy, Rochester, NY
Quong Hop and Co., South San Francisco, CA
San Diego Soy Dairy, San Diego, CA
Soy City Foods, Toronto, Ontario, Canada
Spring Creek Natural Foods, Spencer, WV
Surata Soyfoods Co-op, Eugene, OR
Tofu Shop Specialty Foods Inc., Arcata, CA
Tree of Life, St. Augustine, FL
Turtle Island Foods, Hood River, OR
Twin Oaks Community Foods, Louisa, VA
White Wave Inc., Boulder, CO
Wildwood Natural Foods, Fairfax, CA
Yaupon Soyfoods, Elgin, TX

MEXICAN PRODUCTS

Corn Tortillas:
>Chef Garcia Mexican Foods, Springfield, VA
>Mission Foods, Los Angeles, CA
>Piñata distributed by Alex Foods Inc., Anaheim, CA

Refried Beans:
>Bearitos distributed by Westbrae Natural Foods, Carson, CA
>Greene's Farm, Denver, CO
>Old El Paso Foods Co., Anthony, TX
>Ortega from Nabisco Foods

Salsa:
>Alamo Street, San Antonio, TX
>America's Choice distributed by Compass Foods, Montvale, NJ
>Bread and Circus distributed by Whole Foods Inc., Austin, TX
>Enrico's distributed by Ventre Packing Co., Inc., Syracuse, NY
>Garden of Eatin', Inc., Los Angeles, CA
>Garden Valley Naturals, Burlingame, CA
>Green Mountain Gringo distributed by Home Specialties, Inc.,
>   Chester, VT
>Guiltless Gourmet, Austin, TX
>Hot Cha Cha!, Port Reading, NJ
>Muir Glen, Sacramento, CA
>Pace Foods, San Antonio, TX
>Super G from Giant Supermarkets, Landover, MD
>Tree of Life Inc., St. Augustine, FL

Taco Shells:
>Bearitos distributed by Westbrae Natural Foods, Carson, CA
>El Rio Food Products, Bloomfield, NJ
>Old El Paso Foods Co., Anthony, TX
>Ortega from Nabisco Foods
>Super G from Giant Supermarkets, Landover, MD

Tostada Shells:
>Bearitos distributed by Westbrae Natural Foods, Carson, CA
>Old El Paso Foods Co., Anthony, TX

Wheat Tortillas:
>Cedarlane Natural Foods Inc., Los Angeles, CA
>Chef Garcia Mexican Foods, Springfield, VA
>Garden of Eatin', Inc., Los Angeles, CA
>Mission Foods, Los Angeles, CA
>Piñata distributed by Alex Foods Inc., Anaheim, CA
>Leona's Foods, Inc., Chimayo, NM

MILK AND YOGURT ALTERNATIVES

Rice Beverages:
>Eden Foods Inc., Clinton, MI
>Hain Pure Foods, Uniondale, NY
>Harmony Farms distributed by American Natural Snacks, St.
>   Augustine, FL
>Imagine Foods, Inc., Palo Alto, CA
>Pacific Foods of Oregon, Inc., Tualatin, OR
>White Wave Inc., Boulder, CO

Soy Beverages:
>Eden Foods Inc., Clinton, MI
>Hain Pure Foods, Uniondale, NY
>Healthy Harvest Foods, Inc., Chico, CA
>Imagine Foods, Inc., Palo Alto, CA
>Pacific Foods of Oregon, Inc., Tualatin, OR
>Solait from Devansoy Farms, Inc., Carroll, IA
>Vitasoy, South San Francisco, CA
>Westbrae Natural Foods Inc., Carson, CA
>White Wave Inc., Boulder, CO
>Wildwood Natural Foods, Santa Cruz, CA

Soy Yogurt:
>Nancy's Cultured Soy, Eugene, OR (note: vanilla flavor contains
>   honey)
>White Wave Inc., Boulder, CO

MISCELLANEOUS ITEMS

COCOA POWDER
Hershey Chocolate, U.S.A., Hershey, PA
Kemach Food Products Corp., Brooklyn, NY

CONDIMENTS
Barbecue Sauce:
Annie's Smokey Maple BBQ Sauce from Annies of Vermont, East
Calais, VT
Haddar distributed by Ebba Food Products, Inc., Brooklyn, NY
Master Choice distributed by Compass Foods, Montvale, NJ
Robbie's, Altadena, CA

Lite Coconut Milk:
A Taste of Thai imported by André Post, Inc., Old Saybrook, CT
Port Authur distributed by Gourmet Award Foods, St. Paul, MN
Thai Kitchen imported by Epicurean International, Berkeley, CA

Maple Syrup:
Coombs Vermont Gourmet, Jacksonville, VT
Dancing Star Farm, Charlemont, MA
The Maple River Co., Columbus, OH
Shady Maple Farms, Quebec, Canada
Spring Tree Corp., Brattlesboro, VT
Up Country Naturals of Vermont, Inc., St. Johnsbury, VT

Thai Yellow Curry Paste:
Thai Kitchen imported by Epicurean International, Berkeley, CA

EGG REPLACER
Ener-G Foods, Inc., Seattle, WA
Kingsmill Foods, Scarborough, ON, Canada

FRUITS AND VEGETABLES (CANNED OR JARRED)

Capers:

American Roland Food Corp., New York, NY
Amico Brand distributed by A. Milner Co., Belvidere, NJ
Cento Fine Foods, Inc., Thorofare, NJ
Dal Raccolto, Inc., Linden , NJ
Del Rio distributed by A. Camacho, Inc., Melrose Park, IL
Haddon House Foods Products, Inc., Medford, NJ
Pastore Inc., Baltimore, MD
Peloponnese imported by Gourmet America, Hingham, MA
Progresso Quality Foods Co., St. Louis, MO
Stop and Shop Supermarket Co., Boston, MA

Hot Cherry Peppers:

Bloch and Gugenheimer, Inc., Hurlock, MD
Cosmo's Food Products, West Haven, CT
G.L. Mezetta, Inc., Sonoma, CA
Pastore Inc., Baltimore, MD
San-Del Packaging Company, Hurlock, MD
Victoria Packing Corp., Brooklyn, NY

Vegan Cream Style Corn:

America's Choice distributed by Compass Foods, Montvale, NJ
Del Monte Foods Co., San Francisco, CA
Green Giant Pillsbury Co., Minneapolis, MN
Publix Super Markets, Inc., Lakeland, FL
Super G from Giant Supermarkets, Landover, MD

Mandarin Oranges:

American Roland Food Corp., New York, NY
Reese Finer Foods, Inc., Bloomfield, NJ
Stop and Shop Supermarket Co., Boston, MA
Super G from Giant Supermarkets, Landover, MD

Roasted Peppers:
    American Roland Food Corp., New York, NY
    Cento Fine Foods, Inc., Thorofare, NJ
    G. L. Mezzetta, Inc., Sonoma, CA
    Gourmet Award Foods, distributed by Tree of Life Co., St.
        Augustine, FL
    Mancini Packing Co., Zolfo Springs, FL
    Moody Dunbar, Inc., Limestone, TN
    The Pastene Companies, Ltd., Waltham, MA
    Peloponnese imported by Gourmet America, Hingham, MA
    Sclafani distributed by Gus Sclafani Corp., Stanford, CT
    Victoria Packing Corp., Brooklyn, NY

Water Chestnuts:
    Geisha distributed by Nozaki America, Inc., New York, NY
    Haddon House Food Products, Medford, NJ
    Hunt-Wesson, Inc., Fullerton, CA
    Kame distributed by Shaffer, Clarke, and Co., Inc., Darien, CT
    La Choy distributed by Hunt-Wesson, Inc., Fullerton, CA
    Port Arthur distributed by Goumet Award Foods, St. Paul, MN
    Reese Finer Foods, Inc., Bloomfield, NJ
    Season Products Corp., Irvington, NJ
    Stop and Shop Supermarket Co., Boston, MA

FRUITS AND VEGETABLES (FROZEN AND ORGANIC)
    Cascadian Farm, Sedro-Woolley, WA
    Sno Pac Foods, Inc., Caledonia, MN
    Tree of Life, Augustine, FL

FRUIT JAMS AND SPREADS

American Roland Food Corp., New York, NY
Bionaturae distributed by Euro-USA Trading Co. Inc.,
Pawcatuck, CT
Bread and Circus distributed by Whole Foods Inc., Austin, TX
Cascadian Farms Inc., Sedro-Woolley, WA
Crofter's Food Ltd., Parry Sound, Ontario, Canada
The Dickinson Family, Inc., Salinas, CA
Kozlowki farms, Forestville, CA
Lieber's Kosher Food Specialties, Inc., Brooklyn, NY
M. Polaner Inc. distributed by American Home Food Products
Inc., Madison, NJ
St. Dalfour, France
Simply Fruit from The J.M. Smucker Company, Orrville, OH
Sorrell Ridge Farm, Port Reading, NJ
Super G from Giant Foods, Landover, MD
Tree of Life, St. Augustine, FL
Walnut Acres, Penns Creek, PA

ITALIAN SALAD DRESSING (FAT-FREE)

Mrs. Pickford's Herb Magic distributed by Reily Foods Co., New
Orleans, LA
Pritikin Systems, Chicago, IL
Super G from Giant Supermarkets, Landover, MD
Walden Farms distributed by WFI Corp., Linden, NJ
Wish-Bone distributed by Thomas J. Lipton Inc., Englewoods
Cliffs, NJ

NUTRITIONAL YEAST

Red Star Yeast, Milwaukee, WI

VEGAN MAYONNAISE

Almonnaise from Food For Living, Eureka, CA
Nayonaise and Fat-Free Nayonaise from Nasoya Foods, Inc.,
　　　Leominster, MA
Vegenaise from Follow Your Heart, Canoga Park, CA

VEGETABLE BROTH

Arrowhead Mills, Inc., Hereford, TX
Balanced Foods Organic Vegetable Bouillon distributed by Tree
　　　of Life Inc., St. Augustine, FL
Barth's Nutra Soup from Barth's Nutra Products, Westbury, NY
Custom Low Sodium Vegetable Base, Alsip, IL
Eatem Foods Co. Vegetable Base, Vineland, NJ
Gayelord Hauser's, Milwaukee, WI
Hain Pure Foods, Uniondale, NY
Organic Country distributed by Edwards and Sons, Carpinteria,
　　　CA
The Organic Gourmet from Scenario International Co., Los
　　　Angeles, CA
Pritikin Systems, Chicago, IL
Seitenbacher from Source Atlantique, Inc., Englewoods Cliffs, NJ
Walnut Acres, Penns Creek, PA

TOMATO PRODUCTS
(Note: Organic brands are listed only. There are numerous non-organic sources for these products, too.)

Crushed Tomatoes:
> Eden Foods, Inc., Clinton, MI
> Muir Glen, Sacramento, CA

Diced Tomatoes:
> Eden Foods, Inc., Clinton, MI
> Millina's Finest, Aptos, CA
> Muir Glen, Sacramento, CA

Tomato Paste:
> Millina's Finest, Aptos, CA
> Muir Glen, Sacramento, CA
> The Pastene Companies, Ltd., Waltham, MA

Tomato Purée:
> Millina's Finest, Aptos, CA
> Muir Glen, Sacramento, CA
> The Pastene Companies, Ltd., Waltham, MA

Tomato Sauce:
> Millina's Finest, Aptos, CA
> Muir Glen, Sacramento, CA

Whole Peeled Tomatoes:
> Millina's Finest, Aptos, CA
> Muir Glen, Sacramento, CA
> The Pastene Companies, Ltd., Waltham, MA

MAIL ORDER COMPANIES

Crusoe Island Natural and Organic Foods, 302 Rt. 89 South, Savannah, NY 13146; (800) 724-2233; available products include grains, herbs, pasta, frozen organic vegetables, beans, condiments, soy and rice beverages, jams, tofu, tempeh, seitan, burgers and dogs.

Deer Valley Farm, R.D.1 Guildford, NY 13780; (607) 764-8556; available products include dried fruit, grains and seeds, noodles, spices, and more.

Dixie USA Inc., PO Box 55549, Houston, TX 77255; (800) 347-3494; available products include soy/rice cheeses, soy yogurt, vegan "hot dogs," tempeh, tofu, pasta, and more.

Frankferd Farms, 717 Saxonburg Blvd., Saxonburg, PA 16056; (412) 352-9500; available products include soy yogurt, tofu, burgers and dogs, tempeh, dried fruit, grains, herbs and spices, udon and somen noodles, pasta, seitan and chicken-style seitan, beans, vegetable broth, soy and rice beverages, jams, tomato products, frozen vegetables, and more.

Garden Spot Distributors (Shiloh Farms), Rt. 1, Box 729 A, New Holland, PA 17557; (800) 829-5100; dried fruit, apple butter, grains, pasta, burgers, seitan, tempeh, tofu, frozen organic vegetables, plus more.

Gold Mine Natural Food Co., 3419 Hancock St., San Diego, CA 92110; (800) 475-3663; available products include grains, beans, pasta, and more.

Good Eats Natural Foods, 5 Louise Dr., Warminster, PA 18974; (800) 490-0044; products available include soy milk, dried fruit, whole grains, plus more.

Jaffe Bros., PO Box 636, 28560 Lilac Rd., Valley Center, CA 92082; (619) 749-1133; available products include organic dried fruit, nuts, nut butters, flour and grains, pasta and tomato products, olives, jam, apple sauce, plus more.

The Mail Order Catalog, Box 180, Summertown, TN 38483; (800) 695-2241; available products include nutritional yeast, texturized vegetable protein, and more.

Mountain Ark Trading Company, 799 Old Leicester Hwy., Asheville, NC 28806; (800) 643-8909; available products include grains, beans, somen and udon noodles, pasta, shiitake mushrooms, plus more.

Natural Lifestyle, 16 Lookout Dr., Asheville, NC 28804; (800) 752-2775; available products include pasta, grains, beans, dried fruit, jams, soy/rice milk, plus more.

Paradise Farm Organics, Inc., 1000 Wild Iris Ln., Moscow, ID 83843; (800) 758-2418; available products include beans, soy/rice milk, dried fruit, grains, jam, pasta, salsa, canned tomato products, organic vegetables, plus more.

Phillips Exotic Mushrooms & Accessories, 909 East Baltimore Pike, Kennett Square, PA 19348; (800) AHFUNGI; available products include fresh and dried mushrooms.

Spices etc..., PO Box 5266, Charlottesville, VA 22905; (800) 827-6373; available products include a huge selection of herbs and spices, dried mushrooms, natural flavorings, condiments, and pasta.

Vegan Epicure, Rebecca Hall Kitchen, 1251 Trumensburg Rd., Ithaca, NY 14850; (607) 272-0432; available products include various flavors of seitan in 8-ounce to 5-pound packaging.

Walnut Acres Organic Farms, Penns Creek, PA 17862; (800) 433-3998; available products include beans, grains, dried fruit, jam, plus much more.

Wellspring Natural Food Company, PO Box 2473, Amherst, MA 01004; (800) 578-5301; available products include grains, beans, pasta, dried fruit, jam, soy/rice milk, plus more.

World Variety Produce, Inc., PO Box 21127, Los Angeles, CA 90021; (800) 588-0151; available products include dried fruit, legumes, grains, dried mushrooms, garlic and onions, spices, herbs, roasted peppers, sundried tomatoes, tofu, and more.

INDEX BY INGREDIENT

INDEX BY SUBJECT AND RECIPE

OTHER BOOKS FROM THE VEGETARIAN RESOURCE GROUP

If you are interested in purchasing any of the following VRG titles, please send a check or money order made out to *The Vegetarian Resource Group*, (Maryland residents must add 5% sales tax) and mail it along with your order to: *The Vegetarian Resource Group, PO Box 1463, Baltimore, MD 21203*. Make sure you include your shipping address. Or call (410) 366-8343 to place your order with a Visa or Mastercard. Price given includes postage in the United States. Outside the USA please pay in US funds by credit card or money order only and add $3.00 per book for postage.

SIMPLY VEGAN

Quick Vegetarian Meals, 3rd Edition
**By Debra Wasserman &
Reed Mangels, Ph.D., R.D.**

Simply Vegan is an easy-to-use vegetarian guide that contains over 160 kitchen-tested vegan recipes. Each recipe is accompanied by a nutritional analysis.

Reed Mangels, Ph.D., R.D., has included an extensive vegan nutrition section on topics such as Protein, Fat, Calcium, Iron, Vitamin B12, Pregnancy and the Vegan Diet, Feeding Vegan Children, and Calories, Weight Gain, and Weight Loss. A Nutrition Glossary is provided, along with sample menus, meal plans, and a list of the top recipes for iron, calcium, and Vitamin C.

Also featured are food definitions and origins, and a comprehensive list of mail-order companies that specialize in selling vegan food, natural clothing, cruelty-free cosmetics, and ecological household products.
TRADE PAPERBACK $13

THE VEGAN HANDBOOK

Healthy Traditions From Around The World
Edited by Debra Wasserman and Reed Mangels, Ph.D., R.D.

The Vegan Handbook contains over 200 vegan recipes including Luscious Pasta Sauces, Lentil Mania, Cooking With Greens, Wholesome Baby Foods From Scratch, Healthy Fast Food for Pre-Schoolers, Light Pancakes and Waffles, Savory Winter Stews, A Bit O' Irish Cookin', Wholesome Vegetarian Dishes of North Africa, A Thanksgiving Menu, Eggless Baked Treats, Vegan Frozen Desserts, Crockpot Ideas, plus so much more.

You will also find information on topics such as sports nutrition, online resources, feeding vegan children, a dietary exchange list, a seniors guide to good nutrition, vegetarian history, and Diet and Breast Cancer.
TRADE PAPERBACK $20

THE LOWFAT JEWISH VEGETARIAN COOKBOOK

Healthy Traditions From Around The World
By Debra Wasserman

The Lowfat Jewish Vegetarian Cookbook contains over 150 lowfat, vegan international recipes. Savor potato knishes, Polish plum and rhubarb soup, and Spinach Pies. Feast on Romanian apricot dumplings, Russian flat bread, and sweet fruit kugel. Celebrate with eggless challah, hamentashen for Purim, Chanukah latkes, mock chopped liver, Russian charoset, eggless matzo balls, and Syrian wheat pudding.

Breakfast, lunch, and dinner menus are provided, as well as 33 unique Passover dishes and Seder ideas, and Rosh Hashanah Dinner suggestions. Each recipe is accompanied by a nutritional analysis.
TRADE PAPERBACK $15

NO CHOLESTEROL PASSOVER RECIPES
Quick & Easy Vegetarian Recipes
By Debra Wasserman

No Cholesterol Passover Recipes is a unique book containing 100 vegan and Parve recipes suitable for Passover. Vegan Seder plate ideas are offered. Be sure to try eggless Apple Latkes and Matzo Meal Pancakes for breakfast. For lunch or dinner enjoy Carrot Cream Soup, Onion Soup, or a Thick Cabbage/Beet Soup. On the side serve Prune and Potato Tsimmes (stewed vegetables), Adele's Eggplant Caviar, Chopped 'Liver' Spread, Sweet Potato Kugel, or Potato Knishes. Main dishes include Stuffed Cabbage, Vegetable Nut Loaf, Layered Vegetable Casserole, Eggless Passover Blintzes, plus much more. And don't forget to serve Fruit-Nut Chews, Festive Macaroons, or Frozen Banana Treat for dessert.
TRADE PAPERBACK $9

MEATLESS MEALS FOR WORKING PEOPLE
Quick & Easy Vegetarian Recipes, 2nd Edition
By Debra Wasserman & Charles Stahler

Meatless Meals For Working People is the perfect book for new vegetarians. It contains over 100 delicious fast and easy recipes, plus ideas which teach you how to be a vegetarian within your hectic schedule using common, convenient vegetarian foods. This handy guide also contains a spice chart, party ideas, information on fast food chains, and much, much more. **TRADE PAPERBACK $12**

LEPRECHAUN CAKE AND OTHER TALES

A Vegan Story-Cookbook
By Vonnie Crist
with Recipes by Debra Wasserman

Leprechaun Cake and Other Tales is a terrific book for children ages eight through eleven. Four fantasy tales with seasonal and multi-cultural themes are included.

Children learn about compassion to animals and humans, team work, and healthy eating ideas. Each story refers to different recipes which are included in this creative book.

A glossary of cooking terms, clean-up and preparation instructions, safety tips, and more are included.

TRADE PAPERBACK $11

GUIDE TO VEGETARIAN RESTAURANTS IN ISRAEL

By Mark Weintraub

Guide to Vegetarian Restaurants in Israel is a terrific resource for anyone traveling to Israel. Restaurants are listed by city and town along with a list of health food stores and vegetarian/animal rights groups. The descriptions also include historical information.

TRADE PAPERBACK $12

VEGETARIAN JOURNAL'S GUIDE TO NATURAL FOODS RESTAURANTS IN THE U.S. & CANADA

Edited by Debra Wasserman

OVER 2,000 LISTINGS OF RESTAURANTS & VACATION SPOTS
For the health-conscious traveler, this is the perfect traveling companion to insure a great meal or the ideal lodgings when away from home. It's also handy if you are looking for a nearby vegetarian restaurant to enjoy a delicious meal.

The **Vegetarian Journal's Guide to Natural Foods Restaurants** (Avery Publishing Group, Inc.) is a helpful guide listing eateries state by state and province by province. Each entry not only describes the house specialties, varieties of cuisine, and special dietary menus, but also includes information on ambiance, attire, and reservations. It even tells you whether or not you can pay by credit card. And there's more: included in this guide are listings of vegetarian inns, spas, camps, tours, travel agencies, and vacations spots.
TRADE PAPERBACK $16

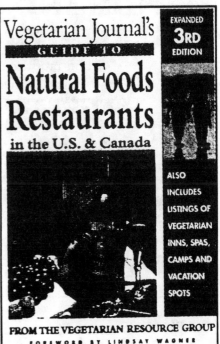

To order additional copies of

CONVENIENTLY VEGAN

send $15 per book to
The Vegetarian Resource Group
PO Box 1463
Baltimore, MD 21203
or call (410) 366-8343.

JOIN THE VEGETARIAN RESOURCE GROUP

a non-profit educational organization
and Receive the Bimonthly

VEGETARIAN JOURNAL

MEMBERSHIP APPLICATION

NAME _____

ADDRESS _____

_____ ZIP _____

TELEPHONE _____ E-MAIL _____

Send $20 to The Vegetarian Resource Group
PO Box 1463, Baltimore, MD 21203
Call (410) 366-8343, fax (410) 366-8804, or e-mail vrg@vrg.org
to charge by Visa or Mastercard.

Don't forget to visit our web site at www.vrg.org